DEVELOPMENT BANKS

Development Banks

William Diamond

THE ECONOMIC DEVELOPMENT INSTITUTE

International Bank for Reconstruction and Development

$3.00

DEVELOPMENT BANKS

by William Diamond

THE ECONOMIC DEVELOPMENT INSTITUTE

International Bank for Reconstruction and Development

THE JOHNS HOPKINS PRESS

Baltimore and London

The Johns Hopkins Press, Baltimore, Maryland 21218
The Johns Hopkins Press Ltd., London

Standard Book Number 8018-0708-5

Originally published, 1957
Second printing, 1957
Third printing, 1958
Fourth printing, 1963
Fifth printing, 1969

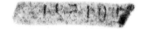

Foreword

By the Director of the Economic Development Institute

THIS IS THE FIRST PUBLICATION of the Economic Development Institute. The Institute was established in 1955 by the International Bank for Reconstruction and Development. Its essential objective is to improve the quality of economic management in government in the less developed countries. At the Institute, senior officials of member governments of the Bank are given an opportunity to study and discuss the practical problems facing them as administrators as well as the larger features of the economic landscape which their immersion in the rushing stream of day-to-day tasks often prevents their seeing clearly. An effort is made to put before them the growing experience of the Bank and of the international community as a whole in promoting economic development.

The work of the Institute has involved the preparation of a number of studies directly related to the special needs of its participants. It is expected that from time to time some of these studies can be published for wider distribution.

Publications of the Economic Development Institute are primarily designed for use by persons working in responsible administrative and advisory capacities in government, financial institutions or other important sectors of the economy of the Bank's less developed countries. It is hoped that they may also prove informative and useful to educational institutions and groups and organizations of all kinds concerned with the problems of economic development.

The publications are the work of individuals. While in every case inestimable benefit has been derived from intimate contact with the work of the Bank, the publications in no sense purport to set forth the official views of the Bank or to be an authoritative statement of its policies in general or in detail.

Michael L. Hoffman

v

Preface

THE FIRST VERSION OF THIS ESSAY was used as the basis for several discussions of development banks in the seminars of the Economic Development Institute. It was, indeed, written for that purpose. No satisfactory book, chapter or article which set forth the main issues and could be used as a springboard for a useful discussion could be found, and something had therefore to be written specifically for the seminars.

The inadequacy of the printed material on development banks is particularly surprising in view of the fact that they are not a new device, they exist throughout the world and there is a tremendous and continuing interest in them. Every country represented at two courses of the Institute has at least one institution which is considered a development bank or is actively concerned with creating such an institution. Hardly a country in Asia or in Latin America does not have one, and they may also be found in the advanced countries of Western Europe, North America, South Africa and Australia. In consequence there is a broad background of experience of development banks on which underdeveloped countries can draw, not only from their underdeveloped neighbors, but from advanced countries as well.

One of the interesting conclusions to which one is driven after examining a sample of these many development banks is that—whether in the United States or in Indonesia, whether in Great Britain or in Mexico—the factors which lead to their creation and the problems they face, once set up, are generally similar in kind, if not in intensity. Of course financial institutions reflect their environment and their times; and it is not surprising that, while the bare bones of one development bank may look much like those of another, one may work well and the other not at all, or at least quite differently. To draw useful lessons from experience thus requires, not only detailed knowledge of how development banks work, but also a separation of the essentials of the institutions from the effects of the specific environment in which they occur or are to be set up. The essentials, often brief and simple when known, are usually difficult to come by.

There is no shortage of general statements about the role and functions of development banks. Nor is there a shortage of descriptive material on the statutes, financial and administrative structures and financial results of specific development banks. Such information may be obtained from their charters and annual reports. Unfortunately this information is not always very informative. It does not always provide the kind of information needed by, say, a Thai or Bolivian official who is interested, not in the Nacional Financiera of Mexico itself, but in the lessons he might learn from its experience, and who does not have time to study two dozen development banks but would like to know what the sum of their experience might mean for him. He is asking himself, Do we need a development bank? What can it do for us? What is the most appropriate way to set it up? What problems will we meet in setting it up and in running it effectively? How are these problems being met by others? Help in answering these questions will come from a detailed examination of operating experience, not from a survey of charters and balance sheets. For it is after the creation of a development bank that the thorniest problems arise; and it is the operating procedures and decision-making process, much more than its capital structure and its organization chart, that provide the clues to why a development bank is or is not doing its job.

Studies of actual operation are few and far between, and by and large they are concerned with the institutions of advanced rather than of underdeveloped countries. Fortunately the International Bank for Reconstruction and Development is engaged in closing this gap. Ten years of experience have led the Bank to appreciate the importance attached to development banks in underdeveloped countries, the role they can play in stimulating economic growth and the need for careful case studies. To facilitate the comparison and cross-fertilization of experience in various parts of the world, dealt with by different departments of the Bank, coordination of work on development banks has been vested in a single Office; and that Office has launched a program of work which should result, in a year or two, in both a systematic treatment of development banks generally and a series of specific case studies drawn from many countries. The International Cooperation Administration, which—with its predecessors—has often used development banks to channel United States aid into private enterprise, has under way a study which is likely to throw more light on the operations of development banks. The United Nations, too, has authorized a systematic examination of such institutions. The prospects are therefore good that before long much more will be known than is known today about what makes development banks tick.

In the meantime, or at least until something better is done, this essay is meant to stimulate thought on the subject and to provide some practical guidance to people in underdeveloped countries. It is a stopgap. It is based on a general view of development banks but on detailed knowledge of only a very few. It attempts to combine the general and the particular in a way that will not satisfy everyone. It raises many questions and problems but leaves them unanswered and unsolved, for answers and solutions are more likely to be governed by specific circumstances than by general principles. It reflects the conviction that, although experience does not by any means solve all problems, its value can be very great if it is properly understood; and it reflects the further conviction that development banks cannot be fruitfully discussed in isolation from the many other institutions and factors related to economic development. These convictions can get out of hand, for they may lead to the temptation to deal more broadly with the subject of economic development than is strictly necessary and to go back to the Industrial Revolution for origins and experience. In this essay the temptation has perhaps not been resisted as completely as it might have been, but the lapse may not be serious if the essay does not stray from the relevant and the

Acknowledgements

ALMOST ANY DOCUMENT prepared for or emerging from the discussions of the Economic Development Institute is, in many respects, a collective document. This essay in particular has had the benefit of suggestions and criticism from my colleagues on the staff of the Institute, from the participants who attended the first two courses of study, from many of the staff of the World Bank and from some of my friends outside it. Their comments and warnings have saved me from many a pitfall, and it is no fault of theirs if I have stepped into others.

Those who so kindly helped and corrected me will forgive me if I do not mention each by name. The list would be too long. But I cannot refrain from expressing my very great indebtedness and gratitude to Mr. A. K. Cairncross, the first Director of the Institute, and to Mr. John H. Adler of its staff who, in addition to giving valuable advice, have had to bear with me since I wrote the first word. I must also thank, for the time and care they devoted to my earlier drafts, Messrs. Richard H. Demuth, Robert L. Garner, Michael L. Hoffman and K. S. Krishnaswamy. Finally, I am grateful to Mrs. Shirley Boskey for her meticulous editorial review of the manuscript. Probably none and certainly not all of these (and of those not mentioned) will agree with everything that follows. They have at least the consolation of knowing that their advice and assistance made substantial contributions to the essay.

W. D.

Table of Contents

What Is a
Development Bank?

IN THE PAST 25 YEARS, the governments of an increasing number of underdeveloped countries have created or have promoted the organization of "development corporations" and "development banks." Those institutions have taken forms so diverse that, despite frequent similarity of formal title, they often have little resemblance to each other and often have little in common. Among them are such different institutions as the Etibank of Turkey, created to exploit mineral resources and to build power plants on behalf of the Government; the Corporación de Fomento de la Producción of Chile, created to draw up and carry out a general plan to promote production in all sectors of the economy and to obtain credit from abroad; and the Industrial Credit and Investment Corporation of India, established to provide long-term finance to private industry. Although all such institutions have been sponsored by governments, which exert a varying degree of influence on their policies and operations, some are owned exclusively by government, others by private interests and still others by a combination of the two. Some are devoted to the promotion and financing of government enterprises, others exclusively to private investment and still others act in both fields. Some have broad planning functions, some can only lend, some can lend and take equities and some can set up and manage enterprises on their own account. Some are concerned with the entire economy, others with but a single sector. Some are regional, others national. Ownership, sources of finance, degree of dependence on government, objectives and methods of operation differ over a broad range of possibilities.

1

A distinction is often made (by the United Nations, for instance) between a "development bank" or "finance corporation," defined as an institution "concerned primarily with long-term *loan* capital," and a "development corporation," which is "concerned primarily with *equity* capital" and with "fostering and managing specific companies as well as providing financial support." This distinction may be conceptually valid but is usually too blurred to be useful in practice. In some cases, banks or corporations created to invest in both loans and equity have gradually moved, in their actual operations, to one or the other end of the spectrum; and others, created to serve one purpose, have evolved in a quite contrary direction, as a result of changing circumstances or shifting government policy. Moreover, in the area between outright debt and common shares lies a broad range of useful investment possibilities. All these possibilities can be of great importance in the stimulation of a capital market, which is another objective of many development banks.

Although the distinction between loan-providing development banks and equity-providing development corporations may be blurred, it does help to point up the two objectives common to virtually all such institutions: the provision of capital and the provision of enterprise[1] when either or both of those requisites of economic growth is thought to be lacking. Though the emphasis may sometimes be on one and sometimes on the other, the purpose of setting up a development bank or corporation is usually to supply

[1] The term "enterprise" will appear frequently hereafter and it would be well to say now what it is intended to mean. Much has been said and written about "enterprise" and "entrepreneurs" and many distinctions have been drawn between the various guises in which they appear, the functions they perform and the conditions under which they thrive. For some purposes such distinctions may be important and useful. However, for the discussion of development banks in the present context, they are unnecessarily fine. It should be sufficient to rely on Noah Webster. "Entrepreneur" is defined as "one who assumes the risk and management of business." "Enterprise" is defined as "an undertaking, esp. one which involves activity, courage, energy or the like; an important or daring project; a venture" and as "the character or disposition that leads one to attempt the difficult, the untried, etc." In short, enterprise (when not used in the simple sense of an undertaking) involves the willingness to assume risks in undertaking an economic activity, particularly a new one, though not necessarily an unknown one. It may involve an innovation, but not necessarily so. It always involves risk-taking and decision-making, although neither risks nor decisions may be of great significance.

these two factors of production in order to speed up the process of development.

There is another, more useful line that can be drawn in considering development banks: between those concerned with government investment and those concerned with the private sector. In some countries, governments have decided that the government itself should—or that only it could—fill the gaps of capital and enterprise required for the creation of new productive facilities. Those governments created institutions to plan, finance and carry out investment projects or programs on government account. Thus the Soviet Prombank, concerned with the long-term financing of industry, is the channel through which budgetary appropriations and other planned allocations of funds are made available to state enterprises. The Sümerbank of Turkey concentrated on establishing, financing and managing industrial enterprises on behalf of the government. The Corporación Boliviana de Fomento devoted itself largely to financing highway construction and a government-owned petroleum production authority. The development banks in underdeveloped countries established in earlier years were often primarily agents for executing government investment projects. Some were also given responsibility for "planning" economic development, presumably in order to remove "planning" from direct political influence, shield it from administrative instability and free it from bureaucratic red tape. It is interesting to note that some of the institutions which were given such broad functions did not in fact carry them out and have gradually lost them or given them up to other agencies of the government.

These institutions sometimes reflected an ideological or dogmatic attitude towards the role of the state in economic activity generally or in particular fields, and sometimes reflected the pragmatic conclusions drawn from the circumstances of the country. In either event they were not primarily investment institutions. The decision to create them centered on the question whether state enterprises should be established within the normal governmental organization or as separate and autonomous entities—on the desirability of establishing a government corporation to carry out certain governmental responsibilities rather than discharging them within the regular departmental framework. The problems raised by the decision to take such functions out of routine government departments are not problems of entrepreneurship or of financing but of governmental organization and administration. Such problems—how to assure responsibility to the legislative and executive arms of the government and to the public while maintaining operational independence; the role of the government in the decisions of the institutions; coordination with other government agencies, etc.—may also be important problems for some types of development banks.

It is not with such institutions as these—devoted exclusively or chiefly to the creation or financing of state enterprises—that this essay is concerned. A development bank, as that term is used here, is a financial institution devoted primarily to stimulating the private sector of the economy. This is not to say that institutions of the former type do not contribute to the development of the private sector. Thus, for instance, the Sümer and Eti Banks of Turkey, as a by-product of their activities, have helped to create a reservoir of skilled labor and managerial experience which has been of immense value in the development of private industry and have, indeed, provided some of the top personnel of the Industrial Development Bank of Turkey. But most development banks have been set up as catalysts for investment in the private sector, to provide injections of capital, enterprise and management, not as administrative devices to handle the governments' own investments. Such institutions were designed to be means of mobilizing resources and skills and of channeling them into approved fields under private auspices rather than into the public sector. Their functions are much more closely akin to those of the investment banking institutions of advanced countries, although they are intended to be pump primers rather than simply conduits for the factors of production and they usually have to perform a greater variety of functions. This kind of institution can make a contribution to development wherever a private sector exists and particularly where opinion and policy hold that economic development depends ultimately on broadly based initiative, managerial ability and technical skills and on the opportunity to exercise them, and whenever those characteristics are in short supply.

The development bank, defined as an institution to promote and finance enterprises in the private sector, is not a new device. Institutions to mobilize capital and to promote productive investment have existed for more than a century. They exist today in countries as diverse in background and circumstances as France, Chile, Puerto Rico, Turkey, India, Great Britain and Indonesia. The recent upsurge in their popularity in Asia, Latin America and Africa and the increasing effort to make them more effective instruments of economic development may sometimes appear to be slavishness to a new fashion. But these institutions are in fact a reflection of the growing urge for rapid economic development and of the search for machinery to use where development does not appear to be proceeding of itself with the desired speed. This was the position of continental Europe, as it looked on Britain in the middle of the nineteenth century; it is the position of most of the nations of Latin America, Asia and Africa today, as they look on Western Europe and North America. In the former context the prototypes of the development bank appeared as a financial innovation, with results of crucial importance to the development of several countries. In the latter context that institution is being adapted to new circumstances with hope of similar results.

To say that a development bank is intended to speed up economic development by making capital, enterprise and managerial and technical advice available to the private sector of the economy does not adequately describe the range and depth of its operations. What exactly is a development bank meant to do? What are the conditions affecting private investment with which it is designed to deal? How much can it do?

The Process of Investment

INVESTMENT LIES AT THE HEART of economic development. It is not the only requisite for development, for development may also come about as a result of an increase in the labor force or a strengthening of economic incentives or the spread of literacy and technical knowledge or a change in economic institutions and organization. Moreover, one may argue about whether a rising level of income is the cause or the consequence of increasing investment; for the very fact that income grows, whatever the reasons, will itself create a need for new investment. In any case, income and capital move hand in hand and investment is essential to the process of development.

Ingredients of Investment

In that process, finance is required for two purposes. It is required in long-term form for the creation or acquisition of fixed assets such as land, buildings and machinery. It is also needed in short-term form, though no less permanently, to be used as working capital, to tide an enterprise over a "season" or a production process or to finance inventories. With economic growth, the need for both types of finance increases.

The traditional association of long-term finance and fixed assets on the one hand and of short-term finance and inventories, on the other, and the traditional sharp distinction between long-term and short-term finance, are not always clear-cut or real. For the finance required to raise and maintain at an appropriate level the stock of raw materials required for processing may be considered long term;

7

and in a growing enterprise the finance required to replace a machine or to expand a plant may be obtained or desired on medium term. Short-term credit may be used for long-term investment; indeed, the provision of short-term loans which are renewed indefinitely is a practice not uncommon in developed as well as underdeveloped countries. Moreover, short- and long-term financial resources are to some extent interchangeable; for an enterprise which can borrow the former may in the process be able to release some of its own resources for long-term investment.

Thus, in India, a special Committee on Finance for the Private Sector found that

> a part of the advances of commercial banks to industries for purposes of working capital, though ostensibly short-term, is allowed to be renewed from time to time. It is a matter of common experience that although these advances which are largely in the form of cash credits are given for the purpose of requirements of working capital, a part of these facilities operate to release the borrowers' funds for long-term expenditures. Though this part of the finance revolves or rolls over, in actual effect it does serve the needs of providing finance for long periods to a certain extent.[1]

On the other side of the world, a World Bank consultant found a similar situation in Colombia.

> Short-term commercial credits have been resorted to by industrial corporations to carry inventories and to finance operations often upon the understanding by the lending institution as well as by the borrowers that credits would be renewed. In this roundabout way, commercial credit has become an imperfect substitute for long-term industrial capital.[2]

In Europe, a special report sponsored by the European Productivity Agency of the Organization for European Economic Cooperation (OEEC) called attention to the "illusory" character, not always recognized "by practical bankers," of the distinction between "provision of credit and provision of capital."[3]

---

[1] *Report of the Committee on Finance for the Private Sector* (Bombay, 1954), p. 45.
[2] *Report on the Colombian Capital Market Submitted by Alfonso Manero to the International Bank for Reconstruction and Development*, unpublished, Washington, D. C., July 1952, pp. 10-11..

Although the line between fixed and working capital, between short- and long-term funds, is not always clear-cut, it is important to make the distinction, especially in dealing with countries where capital is scarce and where long-term expectations are considered so uncertain that available resources are used in ways which permit quick withdrawal or liquidation. There the money market may be adequate while the capital market is narrow and insufficient. "Business" may have all the financial facilities it needs while "investment" is seriously hampered.

The process of investment is not a simple one, for it involves saving out of current income and the risking of that saving in some productive effort. It implies a level of individual income high enough to permit savings, a willingness to forgo or an ability to force others to forgo some consumption today for more income and hence more consumption tomorrow, and the presence of persons or institutions (private or public) who are prepared to take advantage of opportunities for investment and to risk those savings in expansion and in new activities. It implies also that the persons or institutions concerned will have the managerial, administrative and technical experience necessary to use effectively the capital they risk.

A large part of investment is carried out directly by those who save—by the farmer who clears a field or the producer who plows back his profits or a government which applies a part of its taxes to building new roads. This is an important way of saving and investing, not only in underdeveloped countries but also in advanced countries. But another part of investment results from a transfer of savings from those who save to those who invest. This transfer takes place through that complex of institutions called the capital market, to which individuals, firms or governments may resort. A capital market implies not only intermediary institutions, such as banks, insurance companies, investment trusts, issue houses, stock exchanges, etc. It also implies the existence of savers (including business corporations) willing to entrust their savings (or surplus funds) to others in return for interest or profit, and of potential investors willing to borrow or otherwise to obtain the savings of others for a price.

---

[3] *The Supply of Capital Funds for Industrial Development in Europe* (Paris, 1957), pp. 19-40.

The Entrepreneur and His Environment

In underdeveloped countries one or all of these requisites for investment is often lacking. Attention is usually concentrated on the shortage of capital, for that shortage is often considered the main obstacle to development. This is, of course, neither always nor everywhere the case, although individuals and individual enterprises, at all times and everywhere, may be hard put to it to find the capital they need. When people live on the fringe of subsistence, their savings may be insufficient. But they are never non-existent; and it is difficult to avoid the conviction that in many underdeveloped countries savings are in fact higher than they are thought to be, and that more could be mobilized for productive investment. Relevant in this connection are the hoards accumulated from past savings, the often heavy expenditure for ceremonial purposes, the many ways in which savings are wasted or left idle or used "unproductively"; in short, the failure of savings and accumulated wealth to contribute to capital formation.

As the United Nations put it in one report,

> if the other factors are available and the economic climate not too unfavorable, local capital sometimes responds with unexpected readiness to the initiative of local entrepreneurs. The first large iron and steel plant in India for example . . . was financed entirely by domestic capital, collected in three weeks from large and small savers, after the entrepreneur J. N. Tata had failed to raise the requisite £1,630,000 on satisfactory terms in London.[4]

In Pakistan, in 1954, despite the widespread conviction that it would be impossible, the government-owned Industrial Development Corporation was able to sell with ease more than half the equity in its paper mill to private investors. More recently, a World Bank mission to India reported that "in many underdeveloped countries, including India, the amount of capital available for investment is often surprisingly and inexplicably large" and that "very few of the many businessmen consulted by the mission on this subject [of

---

[4] United Nations, *Processes and Problems of Industrialization in Underdeveloped Countries* (New York, 1955), p. 38.

industrial investment] appeared to regard financing as a serious problem."[5]

A low level of investment may thus be the upshot, not only of poverty but of social values or of economic environment which direct savings into unproductive uses, or of inadequate opportunities to use savings productively.[6] In such circumstances, economic development may be not so much a matter of increasing savings as of changing the existing pattern of investment and directing savings into more productive channels. For growth often depends "more on where and how" capital is invested "than on the absolute quantity of savings."[7]

The term "productive investment" has been used here. Observers of entrepreneurs, having in mind the need for economic growth and the kinds of socially useful investment conducive to it, are prone to condemn entrepreneurs in underdeveloped countries for their "unproductive" activities, their persistence in traditional lines of activity and their lack of "initiative." These characteristics are often contrasted to the "rationality" of European or American entrepreneurs who, led on by the quest for profits, display initiative in the creation of new enterprises. Governments often profess this view of their own citizens as a justification for undertaking themselves what is not otherwise being done. The fact is, of course, that it is difficult to find a country in which most people do not act rationally in terms of their own goals and knowledge. It is equally difficult to find one in which people are not pursuing profit actively and directing their savings into channels which the circumstances make rational and which are highly productive in terms of individual incentives. In the conditions prevailing in many underdeveloped countries—instability of governments and of government policy, changing (and often declining) value of money, unskilled labor force, lack of experience with modern techniques, limited markets—it is rationality, not the

---

[5] *Current Economic Position and Prospects of India*, unpublished, AS-54a, Washington, D. C., August 1956, p. 77.

[6] See Charles Wolf, Jr. and Sidney C. Suffrin, *Capital Formation and Foreign Investment in Underdeveloped Areas* (Syracuse, 1955), Chapter II.

[7] Thomas C. Cochran, "The Entrepreneur in American Capital Formation," in National Bureau of Economic Research, *Capital Formation and Economic Growth* (Princeton, 1956), p. 372.

reverse, that keeps most investment channeled in the traditional fields of real estate, commodity speculation and foreign trade. These are the fields in which the investor can find the security, profitability and liquidity which justify his investment. The banking community, of course, works with the same short time-horizon. [8]

The whole range of circumstances affecting the expectations of enterprise makes up what the Indian Committee on Finance for the Private Sector called "economic climate."

> It is a truism [the Committee reported] that while lack of finance might inhibit investment, an increase in the supply of finance will not by itself bring about an increase in investment. Cheap or plentiful credit cannot *per se* be an incentive. Private investment will come forth only if there is an expectation of reasonable compensation for the risks it has to undertake. The investor's expectations of the returns he is likely to get on his investment are colored not only by the purely economic factors of demand and costs but also by various political, social and psychological elements that make up the environment in which he has to function. These semi- or non-economic factors could well limit his willingness to invest and undertake risks, even when a proposition seems worthwhile on purely economic considerations. [9]

Given the appropriate climate (including generally accepted goals which can be attained by economic activity; access to capital, labor and skills; opportunity to enter an industry, etc.), entrepreneurs can emerge quickly in an environment in which they were hitherto conspicuous for their paucity or timidity. This was the case in France in the middle of the nineteenth century, in Russia toward the end of that century, in Mexico during World War II, in Turkey shortly thereafter.

Willingness and ability to change prevailing habits are important because economic development normally entails going into new

[8] See Henry G. Aubrey, "Investment Decisions in Underdeveloped Countries," and Marion J. Levy, Jr., "Some Social Obstacles to 'Capital Formation' in 'Underdeveloped Areas' ", in *Capital Formation and Economic Growth*, pp. 397-520; Aubrey, "Industrial Investment Decisions: A Comparative Analysis," *The Journal of Economic History* (1955) XV, 335-51; and Benjamin Higgins' criticism of the foregoing in *The Journal of Economic History* (1956) XVI, 350-55.

[9] *Report*, p. 14.

activities, notably into industry. It requires not only an expansion of customary activity, of agriculture and of trade, particularly internal trade, but also the growth of transport facilities and public utilities, of manufacturing and mining. The entrepreneur is called upon not only to expand his existing activity but, more important, to enter a relatively or entirely new field: a field demanding technical and managerial knowledge which he does not have and labor skills which his country does not have; demanding larger total investment and a large fixed investment; perhaps yielding lower profits in its early stages if not combined with other new activities for which responsibility rests elsewhere; and this in a market whose size may be small and whose stability may be uncertain. In short, the entrepreneur is called upon to enter a field of activity much riskier and at first perhaps less profitable than the normal activities of the business community.

The bankers share the customary inhibitions of the rest of the business community and are as likely to be reluctant to finance industry as the businessmen are to enter that field. Such capital as is mobilized and made available is usually available only to the traditional, well-known activities and for only short periods. Very often in underdeveloped countries there is no significant shortage of short-term credit, for which the demand and hence the returns are always very great although the terms on which it is available may be onerous. Commercial banks, families and individual money-lenders are usually able to provide most if not all the credit that is required for ordinary commercial purposes. But it is the common experience that they do not provide it for long-term investment or for new forms of economic activity, particularly if there is a long delay before a return is realized. In this the bankers of underdeveloped countries follow the principles if not the practice of the advanced countries from which they imported their banking institutions.

Mobilization of Savings

Another problem that arises concerns the size and hence the cost of the new investment. The largest concentrations of capital are needed for highways, railways, electric power, irrigation and other public works. The capital required for these fields is usually far beyond the reach or interest of any single person or group. Indeed, they are likely to be marked out for government initiative and action, and financed from the capital the government can mobilize through taxation and borrowing. But they are, to a large extent, only means to the production of goods, in both primary and secondary industries which generally depend on private initiative. Mining and industrial enterprises normally call for larger outlays of capital per enterprise and per man than the entrepreneurial community may be accustomed to in its traditional commercial and agricultural enterprises. The initial outlays in such fields may come, as they often did in the past, from the small individual entrepreneur; but more may be needed than he can provide, particularly since industrial enterprise is likely to require new men and not simply the conversion of the older and already wealthy mercantile and land-holding community.

To meet the need for these large outlays, there must be institutions to mobilize savings and transfer them from those who save to those who are prepared to invest. The problem of mobilizing savings is particularly serious where new forms of economic activity are involved, as in the expansion of industry in an underdeveloped country, for savings tend to move within the sector in which they are generated. The industrial sector, by definition small and incapable of producing quickly the resources it needs, must look elsewhere, particularly to the commercial sector. In the course of economic development, industrial enterprise has come from many segments of the community (and chiefly from the merchants) in which capital and skill grew by slow accretion. Where development is just starting, or occurring rapidly, the industrial entrepreneur often has little or no savings accumulated from earlier profits and must resort to family, friends or institutions for his capital. Family and friends, the traditional stand-bys, have the advantage sometimes of being more venturesome because less careful; an institution tends to have what Lord Piercy, chairman of the Industrial and Commercial Finance Corporation, called an "institutional conscience" and hence is "a less comfortable sleeping partner than the private person."[10] But transferred or institutional savings are particularly important because

[10] From address on "The Provision of Capital for Industry," October 11, 1950, cited in Brian Tew, "The I.C.F.C. Revisited," *Economica* (1955), XXII, 225.

they result in broadening the range of investment that can be financed and they improve the utilization of resources. Unfortunately, under-developed countries are characterized by the absence or inadequacy of institutions which can mobilize and transfer savings.

The institutions required to mobilize, transfer and invest savings are not simply organizations to collect and disburse funds. Legal codes and practices are also involved. Savers and investors may require certain safeguards before transferring savings to others or investing them in enterprises operated by others. These safeguards include sound banking practices and protective regulations, laws which permit and facilitate limited liability and corporate organiza-tion, an administration of law and justice that inspires confidence, the existence of persons or institutions to facilitate the transfer of rights and interests. An investor may be concerned about the mar-ketability of the real assets lying behind the security he holds, which also depends in part on legal codes, on the provisions which bear on legal title and which permit or restrict the sale of land, fixed capital, goods, etc. These in turn may be linked to the laws of inheritance, the family system and land registration. There is the further problem of the existence of a market for the assets. Even if they may legally be sold, will there be someone to buy them? Moreover, adequate laws and institutions are not in themselves sufficient. The entrepreneur must be willing to make use of them; for instance, he must be willing to use the corporate form and in large enterprises to permit the distribution of equity. This may not always be the case; indeed, it rarely is in underdeveloped countries, where the tradition of indi-vidual or family ownership is very strong.

The laws, institutions and practices referred to here are those required to sustain a capital market. The institutions include savings banks, commercial banks, stock exchanges, issue houses, etc. The laws concern security, liability and business organization. The practices involve the techniques and traditions of enterprise and finance. These elements are no less important to economic develop-ment than capital and production techniques. Their underdevelop-ment can be an important obstacle to economic growth. In the face of this intricate network of problems, it is small wonder that in the past government securities have generally been the first securities

to be marketed in most countries and that in some underdeveloped countries today the government is the most important single institution for generating and mobilizing savings.

The problems referred to here arise in quite different ways for different types of investors. Either because pressures have been brought to bear on governments or because special attention is being directed to them for developmental purposes, the classes of investors with which governments are often particularly concerned are the farmer, the small businessman and the large industrialist. To provide leadership and finance to such different groups calls for a variety of approaches and often a variety of institutions. For instance, the cost of administering financial assistance to farmers is very high compared with that in industry; saleable security is often difficult to get; and the transmission of the new techniques required to make effective use of financial resources—involving a multitude of families rather than a relative handful of industrial managers and technicians—makes the problem of farm credit quite different in kind from that of industrial credit. Small industries and handicraftsmen suffer from some of these same disadvantages, are notoriously weak in management skills and are sometimes in greater need of working capital on reasonable terms than of long-term resources.

Thus when productive investment is inhibited by genuine shortages of long-term finance, those shortages may reflect inadequate savings; but they may also reflect a lack of appreciation of new opportunities or a shortage of persons willing and able to grasp them or the absence of institutions to mobilize savings or the inadequacy of financial techniques and their supporting legal structure. The fact that there are unexploited opportunities for investment despite the existence of savings suggests that the lack of demand for capital may be as serious a bottleneck as the inadequate supply of capital. Indeed, shortage of capital is closely linked in underdeveloped countries with shortages of entrepreneurship, of technical skills in both planning and operating an enterprise and of managerial talent. The lack of enterprise may well be, in a particular environment, the critical bottleneck. The lack of technical or managerial competence in planning and operating an enterprise may equally inhibit productive investment, particularly when the financial resources required must be borrowed

or otherwise obtained from individual savers or institutions. Most likely, the insufficiency or misdirection of investment reflects a combination of these factors, for they are rarely present in isolation. These various shortages and inadequacies, which are not easily relieved and tend to reinforce each other, may derive from many sources and are deeply engrained in the economic and social structure of the particular country concerned.

How Much Can a Development Bank Do?

This cursory review of the process of investment has two purposes:

(1) to stress the need to understand the problems which, in any given country, a development bank must face and is intended to deal with and

(2) to make it clear that a development bank will not solve all those problems and that, indeed, it may not be able alone to solve any of them.

A development bank is designed to supply one or more of the essential ingredients of effective investment. Which? Is medium- and long-term capital in short supply? If so, why? Are the nation's savings too low, or can they not be mobilized, or are they being misdirected? Or is it enterprise which is lacking? Perhaps capital is available, but no one is prepared to use it in productive ways. Why not? Are the businessmen too cautious or are opportunities lacking? And if the former, what holds the businessman back? What are the economic or social or institutional obstacles? Is there insecurity or lack of confidence in the future? What kinds of policies and laws can be formulated to increase that confidence? If opportunities are lacking, is it because of inadequate resources or because the market is too small? Perhaps there are opportunities and persons who want to seize them. Do they know how to do so? Do they have the technical and managerial competence to plan, establish and operate an enterprise in a new field of activity, often requiring the importation of new machines and techniques? The answers to such questions as these will have much to do with the way in which a development bank is set up, the manner in which it is financed, the direction and method of its operation, and the kind of personnel it needs. It follows, therefore, that one of the first prerequisites for the establishment of a development bank is an examination of the specific economic and institutional environment in which it will operate and an understanding of the main obstacles to productive investment.

It should be clear, too, that a development bank, however broadly conceived, is not capable of dealing with all these problems by itself. A development bank is one instrument among many, all of which need to be used consistently and in conjunction. The country's monetary and fiscal policies, for instance, affect the workings of the bank. Selective credit controls designed to influence the movement of funds in one direction or another may work against the objectives of a development bank. Or the tax system may discourage precisely the kind of investment that a development bank is designed to encourage. Or the persistence of inflationary monetary conditions may make it impossible for a development bank to borrow additional resources from the public and may result in the depreciation of its capital. This is not to suggest that monetary and fiscal policies should be governed by the requirements of a development bank. But it should be noted that these policies may place obstacles in the way of achieving the objectives of the development bank, that some conflict is more or less inevitable and that where a development bank is a governmental institution, coordination of its activities with other government institutions and policies is necessary.

Conversely, efforts by a development bank to encourage the growth of a capital market will run into difficulty if the legal codes of the country make conditions difficult for corporate enterprises or if appropriate financial instruments are not available or if entrepreneurs are distrustful of corporate organization. Revision of legal codes as well as other measures may be required, about which the development bank may be able to do nothing directly, apart from identifying problems and directing the government's attention to them. This does not mean that before creating a development bank a government must import a great many new institutions and completely overhaul its legal codes. It does mean that a government which wants to promote economic development should be prepared to encourage the growth of institutions necessary for such development, to provide the kind of legal framework they require and to pursue the policies which will induce the volume of savings and the kind of investment it is seeking to bring about.

Some Experience
of Advanced Countries

IT HAS NOT ALWAYS BEEN NECESSARY for governments to sponsor or create special institutions to help finance economic development generally and the private sector in particular. When the Industrial Revolution started in Great Britain, the main ingredients of investment were present and posed no problems of significance. The degree of industrialization and the level of income were higher than they are in many underdeveloped countries today. There was a significant accumulation of capital, derived from the reinvestment of profits from agriculture, foreign trade and small-scale industry and from the profits of lending money both to the government and to private individuals. The gains of productivity were so distributed as to give disproportionately large returns to the owners of capital; that is, the inequality of incomes favored precisely those classes which were prone to save and had more to save. There was already a substantial pool of entrepreneurs ready and willing to seize new opportunities for the expansion of existing enterprises or the creation of new ones. Although the financing of investment took place largely through the plowing back of profits, an effective banking system did exist, which provided the greater working capital required for a rising level of economic activity. Moreover, the technical innovations which called for new investment in ever larger units did not come suddenly to England. They came in small doses taken by many people over a long period, so that skills, both technical and administrative, more or less kept pace with investment. Finally, long before the Industrial Revolution, political and social changes had assured the entrepreneur both a place in society in which he could hold his own against the traditional social elites of the country and the popular acceptance of his goals and efforts.

In the Nineteenth Century

Given the gradualness of the process of industrial revolution in Great Britain and the ability of the average firm to generate its own investment funds, there was no need for special institutions to provide long-term finance or enterprise. Through most of the nineteenth century, industry

> was, so far as each unit was concerned, on a comparatively small scale; its basis was in the main a family basis, as the names of the great English businesses still show; its capital was provided privately and it was built up and extended out of profits; insofar as it required banking facilities, it found them from the independent banks, often family banks, which in general had their headquarters in the provinces, and particularly in the Midlands and the North, where the new industries flourished. Moreover, there had existed for many years in this country a large class of investors with means to invest, who exercised an independent judgment as to what to invest in, and did not rely as in some countries entirely on their bankers. [1]

No substantial need for external long-term capital in large amounts arose until the latter part of the nineteenth century when the units of business became much larger and when more and more individual firms were converted into corporations. Until that time, investment banking played a relatively small part in the growth of production. By then, the banks had confirmed their concentration on short-term finance, and specialized institutions—issue houses, underwriters, company promoters, investment trusts—had emerged to deal with the problem of providing funds for fixed investment through the issuance of stocks and debentures. This distinction among different types of banking and particularly the commercial banker's shuddering avoidance of long-term commitments became characteristic not only of England, but also of much of Latin America, Africa and Asia where Englishmen took the lead in the creation of banking institutions.

[1] Para. 377 of the Macmillan Report, quoted in Raymond Frost, "The Macmillan Gap," *Oxford Economic Papers* (1954) VI, 184.

The situation of the European countries that followed Great Britain in industrializing was different. The mere fact of following, while providing the opportunity for imitation, also created difficulties. For once the urge to develop emerged, there was a keen desire to do so quickly, to "catch up" with the leader. This was an expensive task, partly because of the high capital outlay required to take over the latest techniques of production and implant them in an economy relatively primitive, partly because of the need to lay down quickly the costly base of overhead facilities (especially transport) essential to rapid growth, and partly because of the conviction that investment in many fields simultaneously was essential to quick development. Sudden increases in the scale of production and investment were necessary in countries seeking to transform their economies rapidly, which had not been necessary in Britain earlier. [2]

The typical unit of business in Europe (and in Britain) remained quite small through most of the century; and while it did, gradual expansion through small increments of fixed and working capital was possible. The small, individual or family firm is still the predominant form of enterprise. But increasingly the requirements of utilities and large-scale industry and the demands of governments made it more difficult for existing individual enterprises and partnerships to expand and for new entrepreneurs to find the original capital stock they needed. The capital required to make the critical jump from a small to a large enterprise or to create a new enterprise on a large scale was greater than the banks could provide, even when they were willing to provide long-term finance. Other sources of capital had to be found.

The conversion of enterprises from a personal or partnership basis to a corporate one made it increasingly possible to attract savings from individuals and non-banking enterprises. However, to be effective, shares had to be not only profitable, but also readily transferable, with the result that stock exchanges proliferated and the volume of their transactions rose considerably. The growth of corporate enterprise and of stock exchanges was not a simple event.

[2] For an elaboration of this interpretation, see Alexander Gerschenkron, "Economic Backwardness in Historical Perspective," in Bert F. Hoselitz, ed., *The Progress of Underdeveloped Areas* (Chicago, 1952), pp. 3-29.

It required laws making it easier to set up corporations, assuring limited liability, effecting ready access to information about corporations and regulating the activities of exchanges. Step by step, in one country after another, such measures were adopted. Their importance was crucial where railways, canals and public utilities were concerned, and in these fields the practices they permitted and encouraged were readily and widely adopted. By the end of the century they were also widely used in large-scale industrial and commercial enterprises. In this process, the banks on the European continent played a most important role. [3]

In the eighteenth century the large commercial houses and merchant banks had begun to enter the field of investment, primarily in government securities. In the following century, with the growth of their assets and of new opportunities for investment, their activities were extended to investment in joint-stock companies, particularly central banks, insurance companies, public utilities and above all railways.

> In England, the great London houses were comparatively slow in entering into the field of promoting business; on the continent, on the other hand, there was hardly a joint stock company of any importance which did not include among its founders one or more of the merchant bankers of Paris, Frankfurt, Cologne, Geneva and . . . London. [4]

European banking houses were thus feeling their way towards new methods of organization and investment so that, when a vital innovation in banking technique appeared in 1822, a long period of preparation and experimentation lay behind it. In that year, the Société Générale pour Favoriser l'Industrie Nationale was formed in Brussels as a joint-stock bank to sell shares and bonds to help finance commercial and industrial ventures; in the thirties it became the main promoter and support of Belgian industry.

[3] See William Ashworth, *A Short History of the International Economy 1850-1890* (London, 1952), pp. 87-102, and W. Arthur Lewis, *The Theory of Economic Growth* (London, 1955), pp. 265 ff.

[4] Translated from David S. Landes, "Vieille Banque et Banque Nouvelle: La Révolution Financière du Dix-Neuvième Siècle," *Revue d'Histoire Moderne et Contemporaine* (1956), III, 211.

But it was in France, in mid-century, that the new technique received its greatest impetus. At the turn of the nineteenth century the French entrepreneur was typically a small businessman, cautious, suspicious of the new and the risky and fiercely independent. His enterprise was a matter of family and friends. The bankers and the banks shared these characteristics with the merchants and industrialists. The well-established businessman with a need for new funds which his own business or friends could not supply, could turn only to his long-established commercial banking connections. The newcomer was hard put to it to supply his needs. French industry basked in the protection of conservative state tutelage, and the businessman held a low place in the social scale. [5]

From this background there emerged in 1852 two new financial institutions. The Crédit Foncier was a mortgage bank designed to provide long-term agricultural loans, though it also entered the fields of urban and industrial development. The Crédit Mobilier concentrated on investment in utilities and industry. The novelty of these institutions lay in their combination of joint-stock organization, emphasis on long-term investment, power to mobilize resources through the issuance of bonds and promissory notes and, especially in the case of the Crédit Mobilier, vigorous promotional activity.

Due to the personality and energy of its founders, the Crédit Mobilier had a quick and pervasive influence on Europe's economy. The date of its creation was significant and not an accident. For this revolutionary institution appeared when, after the Revolution of 1848, a new spirit of enterprise emerged in France. It is significant also that the founders of the Crédit Mobilier and many of the men of influence around Napoleon III were followers of the Saint Simonian movement. This group believed that industrialization was a means of improving the welfare of the masses and that banking had a special missionary role to play in the process. The association of the Crédit Mobilier with ideas of national development gave impetus to its success in France and elsewhere. It is significant, too, that although the Crédit Mobilier was a purely private enterprise concerned above all with its profits, it had close ties to government policy. Some of its

[5] David S. Landes, "French Entrepreneurship and Industrial Growth in the Nineteenth Century," *The Journal of Economic History* (1949), IX, 45-61.

shareholders were high in the social and political circles of the Second Empire; it was a major promoter and financier of the public works— railway building and urban improvement and beautification— sponsored by the Second Empire; it often invested in enterprises which received government subsidies.

The Crédit Mobilier had a short, stormy and not altogether praiseworthy career of about 15 years. [6] Before it died, it had become a model for similar investment banks established in Germany, Austria, Belgium, Netherlands, Italy, Switzerland and Spain, many of which it sponsored and participated in. Everywhere the main sources of capital for the new institutions were the older banking houses, which also usually provided many members of their boards of directors. This participation of the old banks in the new ones was the upshot of the new opportunities the new type of bank offered, both for tapping savings and for profit-making investment in larger and riskier enterprises than the older banks had been accustomed to, would have been able to deal with or would have dared offer to their old and trusting clients. Their participation (though by no means universal) was the easier because of their experimentation with new methods in the previous half century. [7] With the adoption of the investment practices and methods of the Crédit Mobilier, the banking system throughout Europe, west of Russia, played a role in indus- trialization unknown in England. Particularly in Germany, where every facility for its growth existed and the effect of the innovation was greatly enhanced, the banking system became closely associated with industry as both promoter and financier.

It was of the utmost significance to continental industrial develop- ment that this association was not simply through long-term lending. Such loans were important, if not in the size of their contribution to total investment, certainly in their strategic role in certain economic

[6] See Rondo E. Cameron, "The *Crédit Mobilier* and the Economic Development of Europe," *The Journal of Political Economy* (1953), LXI, 461-88; "Founding the Bank of Darmstadt," *Explorations in Entrepreneurial History* (1956), VIII, 113-30; and "Some French Contributions to the Industrial Development of Germany, 1840-1870," *The Journal of Economic History* (1956), XVI, 281-323.

[7] See Landes, "Vieille Banque et Banque Nouvelle," *Revue d'Histoire Moderne et Contemporaine* (1956), III, *passim*.

sectors and in large-scale enterprises. [8] But the banks also shared in the equity of many enterprises, sometimes directly and sometimes through participating companies, and provided assistance in the form of underwriting and floating security issues, of which they normally kept a part. In the process, they contributed heavily to the conversion of enterprises to the corporate form appropriate to large-scale operations. They also stimulated public interest in securities and the growth of other institutions characteristic of capital markets in advanced countries. Moreover, since they generally assumed responsibility for the enterprises with which they were associated, they played an important role in the provision of technical advice and managerial talent. From the British or American viewpoint, they were investment or issue houses as well as banks, relying to a considerable extent on their own relatively large share capital and not exclusively on deposits. Later, as deposits mounted, the German banks increased their orthodox commercial business, but without significantly affecting their role in the provision of fixed capital. Thus they developed the type of universal bank so often contrasted to the British banking system.

One German banker described the typical process in Germany as follows:

> Scarcely a single important company in Germany has been founded without the collaboration of a bank. Whether it is a case of converting a private firm into a limited company, or of exploiting a new invention by establishing a new enterprise, the assistance of a bank is always involved. The Bank examines the situation and, when necessary, obtains reports from experts in the particular line . . . If the Bank, after examination, decides to found the company, it draws up the scheme of financing, determines the amount and types of capital to be issued and then, in some cases itself takes a part of the shares into its security portfolio with the idea of issuing them at a later date. In this way the founding bank becomes at the same time

[8] It is virtually impossible to ascertain the amount of long-term loans given to industry. In Germany, around the turn of the century, banks may have provided about 10 to 20 per cent of net industrial investment; but this percentage includes participations, working capital and loans for fixed investments. See Helen Thompson, *Role of German Banks in Financing Fixed Investment in Industry, 1890-1913*, unpublished, International Monetary Fund, DM /56 /32, Washington, D. C., Nov. 9, 1956.

the issuing bank, the latter functions beginning, however, only with the introduction of the shares to the Stock Exchange through the intermediary of a bank.[9]

The Crédit Mobilier and its successors and imitators, acting as planners, entrepreneurs, financiers and often managers, thus served Europe's need by (a) mobilizing large amounts of capital from other banks and individuals; (b) using that capital for equity investment as well as for long-term lending; (c) promoting new enterprises in basic facilities, mining and secondary industries; (d) lending to public authorities; (e) facilitating the use of the joint-stock company; and (f) helping to create the institutions of a capital market. Indeed, a broad and active capital market was an essential requisite for effective participation by banks in fixed capital investment, for it was the main channel through which they obtained and provided funds and maintained their liquidity. These banks were designed at one stroke to relieve the shortages of capital, entrepreneurship and managerial and technical skills which face countries seeking to develop rapidly. The Société Générale and the Crédit Mobilier were thus the prototypes both of nineteenth century continental investment banking and of today's "development bank."

Europe is a large and diversified area, and it is not surprising that different parts of it pursued different courses in the development of financial institutions and economic growth. Nor is it surprising that in any given area such institutions did not remain static but evolved and changed. In Germany, for instance, after the original close association between banking and industry and the concentration on universal banking, short- and long-term lending functions tended somewhat to separate. In England, where investment banking was later in coming, the commercial banks played a reluctant though increasing and often unrecognized part in financing fixed long-term investment, and the line between credit and capital, the short term and the long term, became somewhat blurred. What is important is that in both cases there developed banks and other institutions which

[9] Dr. Jakob Goldschmidt, Managing Partner of the Darmstadter und Nationalbank, in evidence before the Macmillan Committee, June 1930, quoted in Thompson, *op. cit.*, pp. 15-16.

together provided capital and entrepreneurship where these were needed.

Although the principles governing American banking appear to approximate those of England, the experience of the United States may in fact be more akin to that of continental Europe. Perhaps one difference was that banking activity in America was characterized by the greater speculativeness and wider range of fluctuations that might be expected in an uninhibited frontier community. Until the Civil War, banking often had the direct support of governments; was characterized, by and large, by the conviction that there was a close connection between abundant money and abundant capital; and laid itself open to the not unfounded comment that American enterprise developed so well because the American banking system was so bad.

As in Europe, enterprises were established, at the start, by persons using their own and their families' capital, and were expanded by the reinvestment of profits. Thus "the efficiency of the entrepreneur as a manager had a direct bearing upon the rate of capital formation."[10] But commercial banks played their part, too, by extending to manufacturers and farmers accommodation loans repayable in installments, thereby helping to finance the long-term needs of both industry and agriculture. In this manner they also helped to finance some of the early railways.[11]

With the growth of large-scale transport systems and utility enterprises after 1820 arose a need for large-scale capital mobilization. Commercial banks made an important contribution, often under pressure from state and local governments, by buying securities and by often frenzied expansion of renewable loans; special companies were created to issue stocks and bonds; and state and local governments themselves invested heavily in securities, issuing bonds to raise the resources to do so. As in Europe, investment banking and the securities market grew out of federal and state government security flotations. The rapid growth of that market before the Civil War,

[10] Cochran, "The Entrepreneur in American Capital Formation," in *Capital Formation and Economic Growth*, p. 345.

[11] Fritz Redlich, *The Molding of American Banking, Part II, 1840-1910* (New York, 1951), p. 326.

chiefly in connection with railway, turnpike and canal construction and based in part on the grants and guarantees of governmental authorities, provided the lion's share of the capital required for the American transport system.[12] The participation of governmental authorities in the expansion of public works in the United States was of critical importance where new and undeveloped territory was concerned. It did not require much imagination to calculate the financial return on a railway line from New York to Philadelphia and to act accordingly. But in parts of the South and the West, internal improvements often "required either government enterprise, subsidy to private enterprise, or else extraordinary illusions on the part of the original investors."[13] The decision (by no means un-debated) was for subsidy to venturesome private enterprise and private management, though illusion and faith also played a part, as the London *Times* must have felt in 1874 when it noted the orgy of company promotion and suggested that many railway schemes seemed to run from "Nowhere-in-Particular to Nowhere-at-All."

After the Civil War, as the scale of enterprise grew and the corporation became the normal form of large-scale economic organization, investment banking became increasingly the field of specialists, who acted not only to finance new enterprises but also to promote them. Well before the Civil War, virtually all types of financial intermediaries were represented in the United States. Although commercial banks never entirely withdrew from investment financing, in the latter part of the nineteenth century these other intermediaries became the means of financing most of the country's large-scale industrial enterprises; and by the end of the century industrial securities began to appear in the exchanges, together with the by then traditional government, railway and utility securities. The bankers

---

[12] A large part of the capital involved here came from Europe (especially Great Britain), whose Barings, Hopes and others bought the shares and bonds of American railways and canals as well as United States Government bonds. Foreign capital was also heavily engaged throughout the century in secondary industries and even in the cattle-range industry. Between 1865 and 1900, about 1,500 British companies were established west of the Mississippi, chiefly in connection with railways but also in cattle and sheep raising, mining, lumbering, etc.

[13] Carter Goodrich, "American Development Policy: The Case for Internal Improvements," *The Journal of Economic History* (1956), XVI, p. 452.

in particular took an active interest in the enterprises they helped to finance, though their interest was normally limited to participation in boards of directors and to approval of the management of the companies they created or controlled.

In the Twentieth Century

In the nineteenth century, the banks and other institutions of the capital market, almost exclusively private in origin, concentrated their resources to a great extent on large-scale enterprise. In the twentieth century there has been growing recognition not only of the special needs of larger enterprises, but also of the needs of small and medium industrial enterprises and of other economic sectors. This recognition often has come in the train of a specific widespread economic problem, such as wartime destruction, the need for rationalizing industry, the effects of depression or social needs and pressures, particularly in depressed areas or in the lagging regions of a country. During and after World War I, new institutions were created to deal with these special problems. After World War II, with the resultant demands for income equality, the greater destruction and disruption of productive facilities and the greater gap between savings and presumed investment requirements, the revamping of institutions to provide medium- and long-term finance accelerated and still more new institutions were created.

Normally these institutions have specialized in one particular field of activity, have usually (and, as time has gone by, increasingly) been sponsored by governments, have generally had government aid in the form of share capital or low interest or interest-free loans or guaranteed bond issues, and have often been under government direction or have had government representation on their policy-making bodies. Another characteristic of these institutions, which distinguishes them from those of the nineteenth century, is that they have generally played no important role as a source of equity capital and as promoters and organizers of new enterprises, but have devoted themselves largely to the problems and reorganization of existing enterprises and to the provision of loan capital.

Every country in Europe has seen the creation of such specialized institutions; the list of those in existence today would be a long one indeed.[14] Thus in 1919, the Belgian Banque Nationale provided the capital (in which the Government, private banks and public later joined) for a Société Nationale de Crédit à l'Industrie, to provide long-term credit to industry. In the same year the principal banks of France and certain large industrial enterprises set up the Crédit Nationale pour Faciliter la Réparation des Dommages Causés par la Guerre, in which the Government has since become an important shareholder. The Industrial Mortgage Bank of Finland was created in 1924 by a group of banks and industries with the blessing of the Bank of Finland in order to borrow abroad with a government guarantee funds which they could not otherwise obtain. In Hungary a Treasury-controlled Industrial Mortgage Institute was set up in 1928 to provide medium- and long-term loans. Its relative impotence and the onset of the depression led the Government and private industrialists a few years later to join in creating a more effective Bank for Organizing Industrial Employment, which was intended to counteract some of the effects of the depression by providing medium-term credit. The National Economic Bank of Poland was created in 1924 by the State Treasury (which actually held all the shares) and state and local authorities, to provide medium- and long-term loans to all sectors of the economy and to administer certain State funds for lending. In Italy, the Government set up the Istituto Mobiliare Italiano in 1931 and the Istituto per la Ricostruzione Industriale in 1933, to provide industrial finance. The latter is now a gigantic holding company as well as banker, controlling and financing a large segment of the Italian economy. Other specialized institutions are helping to finance private investment under the program for the development of Southern Italy.

The Bank of England formed the Securities Management Trust as a subsidiary in 1929 and joined with private banks and finance houses in the creation of the Bankers' Industrial Development Company in 1930, both concerned primarily with the refinancing and rationalization of industry through the securities market. For direct lending, primarily to small- and medium-sized enterprises, Credit

---

[14] See International Bank for Reconstruction and Development, *Report on Institutions Concerned with Long-Term, Medium-Term and Equity Industrial Financing in Europe*, unpublished, No. T-4, Washington, D. C., Nov. 30, 1950.

for Industry, Ltd. was created in 1934. The Bank of Canada established an Industrial Development Bank in 1944 to ensure "the availability of credit to industrial enterprises which may reasonably be expected to prove successful." In 1945, to rehabilitate war-damaged industry and to expand capacity, the Dutch Government, commercial banks and institutional investors combined to set up the Herstelbank to provide long-term credit to industry. In Germany in 1949 the Industriekreditbank, A.G. was formed to take over the activities of the Bank für Deutsche Industrieobligationen, set up in 1924. In 1945, the Industrial and Commercial Finance Corporation and the Finance Corporation for Industry were set up by private banks and financial institutions and the Bank of England, a long delayed reaction to the financial gap to which the Macmillan Committee gave its name in 1931.

Despite the proliferation of these specialized institutions after World War II, they appear, quantitatively, to play a relatively small part in industrial financing.[15] Two recent studies suggest that self-financing remains an important—in some countries the predominant —source of investment resources for industry, indeed, more important than it was before the war. Perhaps the renewed importance of self-financing is related to the prevalence of inflationary conditions and to the fact that, almost everywhere, risk capital has been lacking and capital markets remained depressed. Recovery of the public market for securities has been slow since the war and it has played only a secondary role in industrial investment, because of the shortage of investable savings, the competition of government securities, the reliance of industry on other sources of finance and the effect of tax and other policies. The weakness of the security market has to some extent been offset by the expansion of institutional investment, especially on the part of insurance companies and investment trusts, although these are hampered by severe legal as well as prudential limitations.

[15] For a discussion of private industrial finance in post-war Europe, see United Nations, *Economic Survey of Europe in 1955* (Geneva, 1956), pp. 88-113 and European Productivity Agency of the Organization for European Economic Cooperation, *The Supply of Capital Funds, passim.* This and the following two paragraphs rely heavily on these two studies.

The role of banks since World War II varied widely from country to country, depending on the prevailing banking traditions and institutional arrangements and on government policies. Nevertheless, in general the banks were providing industrial capital on a large scale, due in part to the growth of their fixed-term deposits, in part to the demand for industrial capital and in part to the liquidity afforded by the government securities in which most banks dealt heavily. Noting that "the banking systems are fairly generally expected to do more for financing the capital formation of industry than orthodox views on deposit banking would allow," the OEEC suggested that "it might be advisable to concentrate on devising newer techniques for solving the problems involved [rather] than to go on fighting a rearguard action against the trend of developments." Mortgage banks devoted to industry were few, for the good reason that factories and their equipment are not generally considered good security; but in some countries they were not unimportant. Specialized institutions for long-term industrial finance were much more significant, particularly where private savings were inadequate and government participation, either from budgetary resources or from foreign aid, was required. Yet these institutions were limited in their impact by the insufficiency of their resources, their concentration on loan rather than risk capital, their general unwillingness to compete with other banking institutions and their excess of caution in the selection of clients. Here was evidence of Lord Piercy's "institutional conscience."

Throughout Europe a special problem exists for the new and particularly the small enterprise. For these, self-finance is difficult, for while "the market can finance any kind of hope," self-finance "is the privilege of an already acquired prosperity." Neither the public security market nor the regular banking system has been of great value. In both, the older-established enterprises have prior if not, indeed, exclusive rights. The expense of an issue, the fact that the securities are likely to be unquoted or unknown and hence unwanted by the public, the problems of providing adequate security, the difficulty of assessing the enterprise's creditworthiness—all these conspire to exclude the small enterprise from the capital facilities available to the large.

The problem is magnified for the new firm, large or small, the more so in countries where the average firm *is* small. For at the heart of the problem of the new and small firm is the uncertainty or the inadequacy of management; "access to managerial advice, modern technique, and industrial contacts, is even more important to small and medium-sized concerns than access to outside capital; indeed advance along the one line may go far to remove difficulty along the other."[16] One solution is, of course, to raise the capital at second hand, through the specialized industrial financial institutions which are the European equivalent of "development banks" in under-developed countries. In this field the Industrial and Commercial Finance Corporation of the United Kingdom has given an impressive performance, but even this institution has its difficulties and limitations.[17] The individual investor and the private lender remain an indispensable source of finance for the small and the new enterprise.

In the United States, the problems of long-term finance have developed in much the same way. In 1850, the most important financial institutions were the commercial banks. By 1950, the latter held hardly more than one-third of the total assets of financial intermediaries and their supremacy was challenged by insurance companies and pension funds. In the first half of this century, there was no substantial change in the sources from which these institutions derived their funds, but the uses of those funds have changed radically. The major beneficiary of the change has been the Federal Government, whose securities are now the major asset by far. On the other hand, mortgage loans have declined, as has the financing of business, particularly by short-term loans. However, financial institutions have held an increasing proportion of the main types of business assets: stocks, bonds, both public and private, and mortgage and short-term loans. The growth has been particularly rapid in the field of corporate bonds and stocks. Institutions held 86% of corporate bonds outstanding in 1950 compared to one-third in 1900; and in the same years, one-quarter of corporate stocks outstanding compared to eight per cent. This process has probably gone on for a century. The degree to which economic units have had to resort to external

16 OEEC, *The Supply of Capital Funds*, p. 77.
17 On the ICFC, see Frost, *op. cit.* and Tew, *op. cit.*

financing has varied considerably, with the nature of the firm and the times. It appears, however, that from 1900 to 1950 about two-thirds of the growth of corporations and about one-third of the growth of unincorporated enterprises have been financed externally. Financial institutions provided perhaps one-third of the external financing of corporations, but a much larger part of that of unincorporated businesses. [18]

Self-financing appears to have increased in importance since World War II; and risk capital, as in Europe, has been in a relatively depressed condition. The banking system has continued to provide industrial finance to the extent that, under the pressure of swollen resources and under the influence of heavy demand for those resources, it has continued to operate outside strictly commercial business, in the field of mortgage and medium-term lending. Indeed, immediately after World War II, "term loans" (of more than a year, sometimes more than ten, and repayable in installments) accounted for one-third of total business loans and were important for small as well as for large concerns. They have, to a significant extent, been used as a substitute for equity.

As in Europe, large-scale enterprise has benefited most from the activity of financial institutions and the capital market. The private firm or partnership and the small enterprise generally are still in difficulty when they need long-term capital; and efforts to meet their need have not yet achieved any substantial measure of success. Efforts by the Government since World War I and especially since the depression have helped to open new credit channels for farmers, home-owners, consumers and other special groups and have provided additional assistance to the very large enterprise. But they have left the needs of the small industrialist largely unsatisfied, despite the activities of the Reconstruction Finance Corporation, the Federal Reserve Banks and the Small Business Administration on his behalf. It is an interesting sidelight on this financial gap that in the early fifties, 20 per cent of 15,500 small companies considered themselves short of finance and that of these one-twentieth wanted equity, the remainder loans. [19]

[18] See Raymond W. Goldsmith, "Financial Structure and Economic Growth in Advanced Countries," in *Capital Formation and Economic Growth*, pp. 113-67.

In recent decades, a new type of local and state institution has appeared to assist relatively small enterprises. Generally called "development credit corporations" or "industrial foundations," these institutions appeared in the United States during World War I and have burgeoned ever since. Organized on a community basis, they are reminiscent of the state and local improvement associations of a century earlier. In 1948, there were about 75 such institutions in the United States. By 1956, at least 75 had been organized in New England alone, mostly in individual communities but some with regional interest. They have no government financial support. Their capital comes from widespread voluntary subscriptions or donations of local businessmen and public-spirited citizens. They are generally small, rarely have more than $100,000 of paid-in capital, and often have to borrow for re-lending. Most are non-profit institutions, operating as close to cost as possible; others pay dividends. Before 1950, most of these corporations or foundations were set up to counteract the effect of factory shut-downs and unemployment. Those created since then have been concerned primarily with encouraging the diversification of industry in the areas in which they operate.[20]

Their principal activities are buying and building plants for lease or sale, providing funds for lending to or investment in industry and giving managerial, engineering and other advisory services to small enterprises. Where financial resources are required, these corporations generally take greater risks and lend for longer periods than banks would and thus do not encroach on normal banking activities. They take mortgages as security and normally insist on representation on the boards of the enterprises they finance. They often act as intermediaries in arranging for finance from other sources, their technical studies being of help to those who are prepared to lend or invest.

---

[19] Department of Commerce, *Survey of Small Business Finance* (Washington, 1954).

[20] Since 1949, the *Monthly Review* of the Federal Reserve Bank of Boston has published a series of articles, well worth examination, on industrial development techniques and financial institutions. See also U. S. Small Business Administration, *Development Credit Corporations. What they are. How they are organized.* (Washington, 1953), and Rafael Fábregas, Jr., *Development Credit Corporations in New England and Their Application to Puerto Rico as a Device in Financing Industrial Development,* Thesis submitted for Degree of Master of Science in Industrial Management, Massachusetts Institute of Technology, 1955.

On a larger scale, but still for small and medium enterprises, every state in New England has sponsored a "development credit corporation."[21] Their main resources come not from their equity but from financial institutions which have pledged themselves to provide loans up to an agreed amount. In making their investments, they consider reputation, reliability, experience and competence. Collateral is sometimes important, but more stress is placed on job-creation and on the economic effect of a loan or investment on the community. Many loans have been made by banks on the recommendations of the corporations. In many cases, commercial or savings banks have joined in loans (often taking the shorter maturities) and occasionally local development corporations have done so, too. In addition to lending, the state corporations sometimes build and lease plants and undertake business surveys, as a basis for attracting industrial enterprises into the state.

The creation of special industrial finance institutions by governments is not limited to Europe and America and goes back to the beginning of the century. Indeed, when India first began thinking of an institution to finance industry, it turned for a model, not to Europe or America, but to Japan.[22] That model, the Industrial Bank of Japan, was established in 1902 and was deliberately set up on the lines of the Crédit Mobilier. The Japanese Government had already established a central bank, a special foreign exchange bank and a mortgage bank to finance long-term agricultural development (although, like its model the Crédit Foncier, it moved also into the field of urban and industrial finance). At the turn of the century the requirements for long-term industrial finance were considered too great to be handled by the flourishing banking community or by the still primitive capital market. To fill the gap, the Industrial Bank of Japan was created by Act of Parliament.

The Industrial Bank's share capital was subscribed entirely by private interests (including substantial sums from abroad and from the Imperial Household). Its resources were enlarged by loans from the Finance Ministry and by the power to issue debentures up

[21] They have been set up in other states, as well.

[22] See S. K. Basu, *Industrial Finance in India* (Calcutta, 1950), *passim* and especially Chapter IX.

to 10 times the paid-in capital. The Government also guaranteed a five per cent dividend during the first five years. The directors, president and vice-president of the Bank were chosen by the Government from among the shareholders, and the Finance Minister appointed a controller to manage the Bank. The Bank was authorized not only to take deposits and make commercial loans, but to lend on medium- and long-term and to float corporate and government securities. While it was free to subscribe to debentures, it could buy shares only with the approval of the Finance Minister. The institution thus combined the functions of an issue house, a mortgage bank and a commercial bank.

Industrial loans were scrutinized not so much for their security as for the potential of the industry and the record of the company; and this was done by a special technical department. Like its continental predecessors, the Bank in its earlier years concentrated on new lines of activity and particularly on the heavier industries—iron and steel, shipping, engineering and chemicals. Not until the twenties did lighter industries and small-scale enterprise begin to draw heavily on the Bank. In the case of small-scale enterprises, attention was even more heavily concentrated on the creditworthiness and record of the enterprise than previously, the affairs of the client were closely followed and advice on organization and management was freely given.

The Bank's role as underwriter of and subscriber to utility and industrial securities was greater than its lending role; and it provided capital primarily for expanding, modernizing and reorganizing industry, rather than for launching new ventures. The activities of the Bank resulted also in closer association between banks and industry and among bankers, who increasingly oriented their lending towards industry and began to cooperate in the underwriting and issuance of securities.

Just before and during World War II, the Industrial Bank was diverted from its original purpose. Since the War, however, with a large proportion of government equity provided from American counterpart funds and with assistance from the Bank of Japan, the Industrial Bank has reverted to its traditional emphasis on long-term investment.

What Can Be Learned?

The experience of advanced countries in financing industry is by now so great and the number of institutions engaged in financing industries is so large, that the creation of new institutions in under-developed countries ought to be preceded by an understanding of that earlier experience. The Government of India, for instance, has made such an examination several times in the past 40 years.[23] This is not to say that the circumstances surrounding industrial financing in advanced countries are sufficiently similar to those of Asia, Africa and Latin America today to permit the latter to import wholesale the institutions and methods of the former. Financial institutions, like any others, reflect the background, situation and needs of the country in which they appear and they change as economic growth occurs. But it is possible to learn from the older institutions something of the conditions that made institutional financing possible and to learn, too, of a wide variety of devices used for financing and promoting enterprises, some of which might be readily adaptable elsewhere.

Among the more relevant facts that emerge from a consideration of such experience are these. In every advanced country, the major source of finance for private investment has been the plowing back of entrepreneurial profits. Although the main contribution of banks has been the provision of working capital, they and other financial institutions have also made fixed capital available, sometimes directly, sometimes by providing working capital which then released other resources and sometimes by creating other financial institutions to take the risks of long-term lending and other forms of investment. It appears, too, that the orthodox demarcation between commercial and industrial banking has often been honored in the breach; and it is difficult to avoid the conviction that, with proper safeguards and sound management, a mixed banking system can play an important part in development. Probably the aggregate resources provided by banks for fixed investment have been small, but the fact that they were made available at particular times for strategically important

[23] For instance, the Industrial Commission which reported in 1918; the Banking Enquiry Committee of 1929; P. S. Lokanathan's study on *Industrial Organization in India* of 1935; S. K. Basu's *Industrial Finance in India* of 1939.

enterprises and industries gave them a significance far greater than the amounts involved suggest. Their significance was enhanced by their role in converting the small family business into the large corporate enterprise, an event of great importance for rapid growth.

It was not through lending alone that financial institutions made their contributions to development; of equal—perhaps greater— importance was their role as underwriters and investors in stocks and bonds. The latter was possible only to the extent that laws existed and institutions emerged to encourage the use of the limited liability company and to permit the ready transfer of the documents evidencing ownership and debt, and to the extent that entrepreneurs were prepared to adopt the corporate form. That is, the banks were but one among many institutions in a developing capital market. Moreover, where banks and other financial institutions contributed to fixed capital, they also usually provided technical advice and maintained close continuing relations with the enterprises in which they invested.

Despite the importance of both the conventional and the specialized financial institutions, by and large the large-scale and the well established enterprise has been the main beneficiary of the facilities of the capital market except insofar as, even for smaller enterprises, the provision of working capital eases financial shortages in other directions. For the new and the small enterprise, particularly the individual firm and the partnership, have found no satisfactory general solution to their problem of finding institutional finance, either equity or loan. Indeed, such enterprises tend to want no outside equity and this in itself is an inhibition to getting institutional finance. Yet it is from such firms—whose smallness or newness lends uncertainty to the enterprise and its management, whose instability is high and whose business is expensive—that the complaint of financial shortage most often comes. And it is the small firm and the new one which must be dealt with in underdeveloped countries.

In the twentieth century governments have had little hesitancy in creating or giving support to specialized investment institutions when some particular problem has forced itself on their attention; and private banking institutions have found in those institutions a means of investment which prudence inhibited and law often forbade

Problems of
Formation and Operation

THE VARIETY OF PURPOSES a development bank may serve, and the variety of experience in advanced countries over the past century and in underdeveloped countries in more recent decades, suggest that a wide range of problems and choices must be faced in setting up a financial institution to help to stimulate the growth of the private sector. They include, among others, objectives, methods of financing, range of activities, choice of personnel, rates of return and relationship to government and to clients. They are closely interrelated. None can be considered or solved in isolation from the others. Objectives affect the sources of financing; capitalization influences the nature of the risks that can be taken; relationship to clients and nature of activities have a bearing on profitability, which itself affects the sources of finance. Those problems and choices require consideration both of the development bank itself and of the environment in which it is to work.

Should a New Institution Be Created?

The first point to be decided, in considering the establishment of a development bank, is whether in fact a new investment institution is necessary. Assuming that investment is being inhibited by the insufficiency of long-term capital, it might be possible to induce existing institutions to provide that capital. In this event, there might be little point in setting up a new institution. It might, indeed, be undesirable to do so, given the expense involved, the shortage of managerial and technical personnel generally prevailing in underdeveloped countries and the undesirability of spreading that personnel too thinly.

In some cases virtually autonomous departments of the central bank provide long-term industrial finance. In Australia, for instance, it was decided in 1945 to establish within the Commonwealth Bank an Industrial Finance Department, most of whose resources have been drawn from the Commonwealth Savings Bank. Because of some criticism, however, from private banks and the belief that a central bank, to be an effective instrument of monetary policy, should not have general lending functions, consideration is being given to establishing the Industrial Finance Department as a separate development bank.

Another possibility is a formal or informal consortium of banks or individuals, prepared to share among themselves the risks of financing new enterprises. Such a consortium was created in 1949 by Mexican commercial banks and the Nacional Financiera as a means of making available to private industry the foreign exchange proceeds of a World Bank loan. It very soon disappeared, hardly having touched the loan, due in part to the fact that it had no staff, no leadership and no incentive to remain in existence. In El Salvador, a group of well-to-do persons has combined in a consortium to provide capital for sound enterprises. *Ad hoc* syndicates are an old device which has proved its usefulness; but unless there is some organization and staff, a formula for participation and above all an incentive to remain together, each syndicate member is likely to go his own way.

Another method, of course, would be to use the existing banks directly. Commercial banks often participate in industrial financing (or create investment subsidiaries to do so) and they might be induced to go further, for instance by special rediscount privileges as is now being proposed in India, by manipulation of reserve requirements or by other measures of monetary policy, combined with limits on the nature and amount of the banks' resources that could be used for the purpose. Central banks are in a position, in case of emergency, to provide the liquidity required by the banks. The commercial banks have done an appreciable part of the industrial financing of continental Europe and the United States since the early nineteenth century.

Generally this possibility is viewed with suspicion, perhaps largely because of the conviction that demand deposits require a very high level of liquidity and should be invested on the shortest possible term in self-liquidating loans. The history of banking in the advanced countries (particularly during the panics of 1929-33) lends considerable point to this widely accepted principle. In its extreme form, of course, it is obviously absurd and few act on it. The

> banker is able to make a living because he knows that repayment of his deposits is in fact not required in total at any one time, and he could not make any living by matching his assets precisely to his liabilities. On the other hand, he cannot behave like an investment trust. The liquidity he must maintain is a matter of degree; there can be no absolute rule on this ground forbidding the holding of medium-term and long-term assets, and almost every banker of strength and reputation does in fact hold some of these less liquid assets.[1]

The same history that points up the dangers of bank illiquidity also suggests that a substantial proportion of demand deposits is no less permanent than savings deposits, that reserves are often larger than they need to be and that the restriction of commercial banks to self-liquidating, short-term commitments does not serve to keep them from engaging in some kinds of speculative investment when they are so inclined.

In many countries law forbids the marriage of commercial and investment banking, although it is sometimes doubtful that the banks would make longer term commitments even if they could, in view of the large and profitable demand for other kinds of business. Thus Colombia, when the World Bank survey mission visited it in 1949, forbade commercial banks to lend for any purpose for a period of more than a year and to lend at all for industrial enterprises or real estate. Rigid regulations to assure the liquidity of the banking system resulted in a complete separation of the commercial banking system from long-term capital formation and encouraged extensive credit for short-term commercial and speculative purposes, without in the last analysis assuring the soundness of the system.[2] On the

---

[1] R. S. Sayers, *Central Banking after Bagehot* (Oxford, 1957), pp. 121-22.

[2] IBRD, *The Basis of a Development Program for Colombia* (Baltimore, 1950), pp. 303-04.

recommendation of the mission, the law was changed to allow the banks to lend for up to five years for certain economically useful purposes. In Cuba, where a World Bank mission found a high level of both demand and savings deposits and a strong reserve position, savings banks acted as cautiously as commercial banks and the mission strongly recommended an increase in long-term lending. [3] In other countries, too, savings banks and the savings departments of commercial banks are barred from long-term transactions, except for the purchase of government bonds. Permissive legislation may be necessary in such cases as these, but it may not be a sufficient inducement and may have to be combined with the incentives and restrictions implicit in credit policy. Given effective instruments of monetary policy, adequate bank inspection, a central bank prepared to provide discriminating liquidity, and an understanding of the varying liquidity requirements of the different types of resources at the disposal of a bank, the marriage of commercial and investment banking is safer and more effective than the traditional principle would lead one to believe.

The Indian Committee on Finance for the Private Sector recommended a degree of "mixed" banking when it suggested that "the Reserve Bank can facilitate larger investment by commercial banks and other financial institutions in private industry by suitable adjustments in its lending and discounting practices" and that banks should increase their investments in industrial securities, make larger advances against such securities and form a syndicate with finance companies to underwrite new industrial securities. It pointed out that an investment of a mere five per cent of deposits in industrial securities would make available a substantial amount of long-term finance without seriously jeopardizing the liquidity position of the financial institutions concerned. [4] In Mexico, official policy has both inadvertently and deliberately led the commercial banks into greater participation in the capital market. Since there was a limit on the interest rate for short-term loans, many banks set up or merged with private financieras, whose rates were not restricted. More important, the central bank appears to have achieved a degree of success in

[3] IBRD, *Report on Cuba* (Baltimore, 1951), pp. 587-88.
[4] *Report*, pp. 42, 48-49.

directing commercial banks into medium- and long-term loans and into industrial securities. Since 1948, the investments of banks in those fields has risen from 21 per cent to 32 per cent of their total financing, and by 1955 the commercial banks were the source of 20 per cent of all the medium- and long-term financing provided by the banking system. The shift took place under the influence of the reserve requirements imposed by the Bank of Mexico, which offered a strong incentive to commercial banks to extend medium-term loans to industry. This event was to a large extent responsible for the failure of the consortium of banks which the World Bank helped create in 1949; for the individual banks, lured in any case into medium-term lending, could profit more by lending directly from their own resources than by sharing with others the earnings from re-lending a World Bank loan.

The Indian Committee also recommended increased participation by the banks and other financial institutions in development banks and corporations.[5] This is a variety of second-hand investment through which the banks can avoid some of the difficulties of investing directly. The fact is that just as a century ago the commercial banks provided the capital for the investment institutions which were the prototypes of development banks, so in most countries today the largest shareholders in development banks, after governments, are the commercial banks. It has not always been easy to arrange for such investment, perhaps because of the conventional banks' fear that a development bank would cut into or interfere with their ordinary business, and in part because of the existence of more lucrative opportunities. But it is not difficult to argue that a successful investment institution, by raising the general level of economic activity, will redound to the benefit of the commercial banks by increasing the number and business of their clients.

The fear of losing business existed and the argument that business would grow in the long run was used in Turkey in 1950, when the Industrial Development Bank was created.[6] There, commercial banks took up three-quarters of the original equity of the Industrial Development Bank, not because they were farsighted but because

[5] *Report*, p. 50.
[6] For a description of the Industrial Development Bank of Turkey, see Appendix II.A.

of the pressure brought to bear on them by the Central Bank and by
the Government. Their earnings from that investment may be no
greater and probably are less than those afforded by other opportunities available then and now; but the indirect business accruing to
them from the expansion of existing enterprises and the creation of
new ones has been substantial. In Turkey, the commercial banks now
often refer potential borrowers to the Industrial Development Bank
(as in New England they refer borrowers to the development credit
corporations with which they are associated) when the borrowers'
proposals are considered too risky for a normal bank or involve too
long a term. The converse of this practice is not often followed in
underdeveloped countries, though it is far from rare in advanced
countries; that is, development banks might explore, more often
than they do, the possibility of associating other banks with them in
syndicates or consortia for particular loans and investments.

Ways of safely extending the range and term of operations of
existing banks need further examination because possibilities do
exist, because there is a demand for their resources and because more
is expected from them. Yet two factors above all militate against
relying on them directly for substantial long-term finance. The most
important of these concerns the risk and safety of long-term investments, as contrasted with their liquidity. The mentality, tradition and
competence of commercial banking are conditioned by short-term
forecasts and operations, quick turn-over and easy liquidity. The
longer-term outlook required for investment financing is conspicuous
by its absence, as is the willingness to take the risks which the
financing of new enterprises necessarily involves. Moreover, the
inherently greater risks of long-term investment must be dealt with
by special skills not readily available.

> The logically sound basis for the presumption against long-term
> commitments is that it is much more difficult to estimate a borrower's
> creditworthiness twenty years ahead than six months ahead. The
> factors relevant to creditworthiness are substantially different over
> the longer period and the capacity and experience required in the
> bank manager are of an altogether different order, an order it is not
> reasonable generally to expect [unless he has specialized expert staff].[7]

[7] Sayers, *op. cit.*, p. 122.

Secondly, the conversion of commercial banks to long-term financing might well result only in diversion of their existing resources from short-term and working capital lending. This, up to a point, might be desirable. But such loans meet a need as important as long-term credit, from which, indeed, they are often economically indistinguishable. Inventories are often equivalent to one-third to one-half of national income in advanced countries, and in any country a substantial proportion of net investment must go to finance increases of inventories if a shortage of raw materials and finished goods is to be avoided. In a country still in the process of converting to an exchange economy the expansion of commercial credit might be particularly important. An effort to develop long-term capital investment entirely at the expense of the short-term might work against the effectiveness of both.

Thus, substantial efforts can be made to divert more of the capital, reserves and time deposits and a certain proportion of the demand deposits of the conventional banks into long-term investment. Yet the institutional preoccupation and competence of commercial bankers, the dangers inherent in pressing the banking system too far in this direction, the inadequacy or absence of a capital market and the limited effectiveness of monetary policy in an underdeveloped country, are likely to lead to the conclusion that the existing banks will be inadequate to provide the stimulus needed for long-term investment. There is thus a presumptive case in most countries for concluding that a new institution *is* necessary to help to provide long-term investment finance, as well as those other essential ingredients of investment—enterprise and skills.

The Scope of the Bank's Activities

Another question that immediately arises in setting up a development bank relates to the scope of its activity. What sectors of the economy should it attempt to cover? Should it specialize in one sector, or should it provide finance for more than one or even for all? Should it be restricted to a given geographical area, or should it blanket the country? Can it effectively service both large- and small-scale enterprise?

When a government sponsors the establishment of a development bank (this is usual, though by no means necessary), it is likely to be concerned with the several different fields of long-term investment which fall into or at least overlap the private sector. These include agriculture, small industry, large-scale industry, mining and urban housing, as well as transport and power, which are more likely to be in the public sector. A bank could be set up to cover all these fields, or it could specialize in one or more. Thus the Chilean Corporación de Fomento was authorized to cover virtually the entire economy and the Philippine Rehabilitation Finance Corporation was empowered to provide credit for commerce, housing, agriculture and industry, to reconstruct damaged property and to broaden and diversify the economy. Some development banks have tended, despite the broad scope of their charters, to concentrate on one or another field. The Puerto Rico Industrial Development Company, originally set up to aid commerce, mining and industry, has concentrated virtually all its resources on the last. The more recently created development banks have had a narrower scope to start with, being usually limited by their statutes to a single sector. One result has been the creation of several such institutions in some countries, each devoted to a particular field.

Specialization has its advantages. Too broad a scope might, unless financial resources are plentiful, spread them too thinly. The many related activities in which development banks necessarily become involved make it difficult for them to cover the entire economy adequately. The financing of agriculture together with other sectors is particularly risky because of the necessity of locating the institutions serving agriculture close to the farm, because of the special security problems involved, because of the vital necessity for linking loans to extension and other technical services which only a specialized agricultural bank or extension service is in a position to provide and because of its very high costs. Moreover, agricultural credit has become closely linked with social objectives, and may carry a high component of subsidy which could be better provided through other means. Similarly, the financing of small-scale industry is an expensive affair, if it is done wisely and well, with the careful investigation and supervision that are required. In the United Kingdom, the ICFC makes loans as low as £5,000 (about $14,000) but those under

£15,000 (about $42,000) show no profit and may even be losing propositions, taking into account the cost of prior study and subsequent administration and the high risks inherent in financing small enterprises. In Indonesia, the State Bank for Industry has found that it cannot deal with investments of less than Rps. 100,000 (about $9,000), and it has therefore restricted itself to medium- and large-scale enterprises. The Industrial Credit and Investment Corporation of India has decided that Rs. 500,000 (about $105,000) is the practical lower limit of its financial assistance. Of course, an interest rate could be set which would cover the risk and the cost incurred; but in the case of a small enterprise, the risk may be unmeasurable and the rate that would cover both would be unacceptable. The provision of equity instead of loans does not provide a complete answer in this area of investment, for it is precisely in the field of small enterprise that the problems of providing equity are greatest.

The size of enterprise that can be financed on a profitable basis will vary from country to country, but there is a point below which a properly made and supervised loan cannot break even. This is a consideration of primary importance to a development bank whose equity is private and which must therefore seek profitability; such an institution is likely to avoid the small investment in favor of the large. It may be no less important to a government-owned bank, for the government, too, may wish the institution to be at least self-supporting and may find more appropriate ways of providing subsidies to small industries. Thus, in Mexico the Government has established a special small enterprises fund for investments which the Nacional Financiera could not or would not make. In India, State Finance Corporations have been created to deal with small investments which the Industrial Finance Corporation could not handle. [8] Below this level the Government has established a National Small Industries Corporation to work with Small Industries Service Institutes and with an industrial extension service; and still other organizations have been created to help stimulate and finance cottage industries.

Considerations of geography also enter into the problem of scope. They had a bearing on the Indian decision to establish State develop-

---

[8] For a description of development banks in India, see Appendix II.B.

ment banks. In a country the size of Ceylon or Costa Rica there may be no point to having regional development banks. In Turkey, although the investments of the Industrial Development Bank are heavily concentrated around three main cities, there is no part of the country to which its activities do not extend. But in India's broad expanse, the need for intimate knowledge of local conditions and of the local applicants for finance almost forces the creation of regional institutions, especially where relatively small enterprises are concerned. It was this kind of situation, incidentally, which first led the World Bank to assist development banks as a means of making small loans to small and medium-sized private enterprises with which it could not otherwise deal effectively and at a reasonable cost.

In some countries, special circumstances recommend specialization. Thus when the Industrial Development Bank of Turkey was set up, mining was deliberately omitted from its field of operation. This resulted partly from the conviction that the Bank's resources were insufficient to cover both industry and mining, but chiefly from the view that the Government's uncertain policies toward private mining made demand in that sector very small and would have created nothing but trouble for the new bank.

The tendency toward specialization may result in more effective operation but it also produces its own problems. It may multiply the need for administrative and managerial personnel. It may increase risks by concentrating rather than dispersing resources. Where the development banks are government institutions, it may aggravate the need for coordinating bodies to assure that the banks work harmoniously with each other and with government policy.

The Nature of the Bank's Activities

In the circumstances of underdeveloped countries, a development bank can serve many purposes. Capital may be in short supply; then again it may exist but be timid, in which event what may be wanted, particularly in untried lines of activity, is initiative. Savers may need only the confidence that comes from a going and successful enterprise. Even in developed countries, a new enterprise can rarely obtain capital from the public sale of stocks or bonds; securities are floated primarily by successful enterprises. Again, both capital and initiative may be present, but there may be a lack of experience—technical or managerial—to set up and operate the enterprise.

A development bank can, if it is so authorized by its charter, provide capital as loans or as equity or in some intermediate form, for instance in preference shares or at a fixed rate plus bonus stock or a share of profits. Capital is most frequently sought in the form of medium- and long-term loans and loans do not necessarily involve the bank in direct responsibility for the enterprise financed. Lending in fact makes up the bulk of the financial activities of most development banks, except for those (like the Pakistan Industrial Development Corporation) which are authorized only to create and operate new enterprises.

To lend safely is important but not always easy. In normal banking practice, a loan must be secured and the security available may be insufficient to cover adequately the funds required. This is often the case with a new enterprise, and results in the accusation that only the rich can borrow. Sometimes satisfactory security is not legally available, a situation which seriously inhibits agricultural lending in Ethiopia, where it is difficult or impossible to get or enforce a lien on property in some parts of the country. In Ceylon, land titles are notoriously unclear and legal requirements for disposing of security in case of default are so onerous that they limit mortgage loans for industry too. Moreover, security in industrial lending may prove to be illusory. Industrial plants and equipment are considered poor security in most countries, because it may be difficult to realize their value even in good times, let alone bad. The problem may be more difficult in an underdeveloped country than in an advanced one, for in the former the potential buyers are likely to be fewer, especially if the industry concerned is new and unfamiliar.

It is, of course, possible to place too much emphasis on security and too little on the prospective profitability of the enterprise. The Ceylon Development Finance Corporation and many other development banks are specifically authorized to grant loans without security. Indeed, the earning capacity of the enterprise and the quality of its management are of paramount importance in assessing the prospects of repayment. Thus, while a well-run bank (whatever its statutory powers) is likely to insist on security, the chances are that its judgment of the borrower, his character, his background and his experience, rather than the security he is able to provide, will determine whether he gets a loan. This is a sound principle, given the risks implicit in industrial security; but judgment about the borrower at once raises the issue of the prevailing commercial morality and whether a banker can count on the strict fulfillment of business undertakings.

More concern with earning capacity and less with security opens the way to equity investments. Indeed, equity rather than loans is often the appropriate way of providing the required capital. This may especially be the case with a new enterprise or a rapidly expanding one, on which fixed debt beyond a certain level might place an intolerable burden. A development bank ought to be prepared to take equity participation in lieu of or in addition to making loans or to undertake to look elsewhere for the equity required. Some development banks, like the Nacional Financiera of Mexico and the Industrial Development Bank of Turkey, are authorized to acquire the shares of an enterprise, while others, like the Pakistan and the Indian Industrial Finance Corporations, may underwrite shares but may not subscribe to them. The Nacional Financiera makes a particular point of seeking private equity, both foreign and domestic, for all the large projects it initiates.

In many countries, the provision of equity is limited less by the statutory powers of development banks than by the unwillingness of the average entrepreneur to take others into his business and to share his ownership, management and profits, to say nothing of his secrets. This attitude towards personal ownership and control amounts almost to a fetish among the small enterprises of advanced countries as well. The Turkish Industrial Development Bank was able, in five years of operation, to arrange only a very few joint ventures, owing partly to the reluctance of entrepreneurs. Even in the field of outright lending, the Industrial Finance Corporation of Pakistan was at first unable to do much business because it was not permitted to make any investment except in a limited liability company or a registered cooperative. The ban had to be lifted. A partial solution to this problem might be investment in preferred stock, or a loan carrying a low fixed interest supplemented by a percentage of profits or bonus shares. Loans of the Indonesian State Bank for Industry have often taken this mixed form. Lending, too, is often inhibited by this reluctance of the entrepreneur to divulge information about his business, and he may prefer the higher rates of the private lender to the troublesome, prying and sometimes embarrassing questions of a development bank. In such circumstances, which have faced the development banks of Ethiopia and Turkey, reliance must be placed on the gradual establishment of a high degree of confidence between borrower and lender and of an understanding of mutual self-interest. The resistance to equity investment, too, can be worn down in time. In this manner, development banks may be able to contribute to a reorientation of the thinking of entrepreneurs about business organization which is essential to economic development.

Obviously the ability of a development bank to participate in the equity of enterprises will depend on the circumstances of the country and the degree of development of its capital market. In India, Japan and Mexico, with relatively well-developed capital markets and fairly widespread use of the corporate form of organization, direct participation by development banks is possible to a degree still uncommon in Turkey or unheard of in Ethiopia. In the case of Turkey's Industrial Development Bank, the low level of equity financing to date has been due not only to public reluctance (which is decreasing) but to an internal factor that may exist in other privately owned development banks. A private development bank, even if it has large sums of government money, must pay dividends and the sooner the better. Loans may yield lower returns but they will yield them more quickly than equity investments. The Turkish bank therefore decided deliberately to minimize its subscriptions to equity until it felt itself on a fairly sound financial basis and able to pay a minimum dividend from profits—and until inflationary pressures in Turkey led the bank to stress equities as a hedge against inflation. Such inhibitions might not affect a government-owned development bank. Still, even the latter might be under pressure from a short-sighted parliament or executive to produce financial results quickly. The government-owned Ethiopian Development Bank, for instance, has for several years been dominated by the conviction that its operations must be very safe and profitable. As a result, its investments have been much more conservative than they might otherwise have been.

The important point here is that no one type of financial instrument is likely to be suitable to all cases. A development bank ought to be able to adapt its methods of providing finance to the circumstances, keeping its attention and interest focused to the extent possible on the risk involved in, and the potential growth of, the enterprise to be financed.

In some underdeveloped countries, there will be no shortage of requests for loans from the development bank. In Turkey, from 1951 to the end of 1956, the Industrial Development Bank received 1,993 loan applications. In other countries, there has been no such queue. In such cases a development bank may have to undertake a promotional campaign. Officials of the Turkish bank travelled throughout the country in 1951 and 1952 to acquaint banks and potential borrowers with the services the bank could offer. The Puerto Rico Industrial Development Company has been perhaps unique in the intensity of its promotional campaign, both in the United States and on the Island. Promotion is a major activity of the New England development banks. In advanced countries, the investment banks of the nineteenth century always relied heavily on promotion and themselves created a substantial amount of their business. Governments, which today direct most development banks, ought to be no less resourceful in promotion.

Providing capital to others on request, in whatever form, is not likely to be the sole financial activity of a development bank. In underdeveloped countries, even when opportunities for investment exist and are clearly pointed out, the initiative and willingness to grasp them may not be present until it is shown that those opportunities are profitable. Development banks may therefore have to assume the responsibility of establishing enterprises entirely on their own account. This type of pioneering in new fields has been a main objective of many development banks, notably those of Chile and Mexico, although some are barred from such activity. The Industrial Development Corporations of Pakistan and India were specifically set up to lead the way into industries considered vital to the nation, when it was found that the limited effectiveness of their Industrial Finance Corporations was in part due to the necessity of relying on the initiative of individual entrepreneurs. It is perhaps natural that in underdeveloped countries, the pioneering development banks (even though meant to stimulate the private sector) are most often those that are controlled by governments. For it is these which are given development objectives in terms of specific priorities to follow, industries to establish or projects to carry out.

The acquisition of equity, investment in security issues and the creation of new enterprises on its own account are closely linked with the role of a development bank in fostering a capital market. A development bank can help to stimulate a capital market by selling its own stocks and bonds, by helping enterprises float or place their securities, and by selling from its own portfolio as widely and as quickly as possible. These have been among the main activities of investment banks in advanced countries, but only to the extent that a capital market existed or that investment banks were able to foster one. In doing so, development banks face the resistance of entrepreneurs who prefer personal ownership or partnership and the resistance of potential investors who may know little or nothing about securities. They may face institutional or legal inadequacies. In all these respects, a development bank can pioneer, using its concrete experience to convince the government and the public alike of the desirability of the changes in law and custom necessary to foster a capital market.

A development bank does not always have to start from scratch. In India or Japan, the capital market, the concept of limited liability and the stock exchange are sufficiently well developed to permit development banks to use their resources to underwrite issues of corporate securities. In Turkey such an operation has not yet been considered possible, nor has the development bank been able to sell its own bonds to the public. In Mexico, the Nacional Financiera created a new type of security, a "participation certificate" representing co-ownership of a designated group of securities in the portfolio of the Financiera.[9] They have provided a large part of the Financiera's resources, due perhaps to the support of the Financiera, the Bank of Mexico and ultimately the Government that lay behind

[9] See Appendix II.C. for a brief description of the Nacional Financiera.

them. Until the latest issue (1956), they bore fixed interest and were returnable on demand and at par. Despite their widely recognized weaknesses, they were a means of introducing industrial securities to the public. The "participation certificate" illustrates, too, how a development bank can devise a type of security which offers the features a country's investors want. Ability to sell from portfolio will also depend on the record of profitability and confidence which the development bank's client corporations have been able to create.

If a development bank is to sell from its portfolio, its investments must be saleable and they must be made on terms which the market will find attractive. This is another reason for flexibility in the choice of financing. But flexibility may not always be easy. Legal codes may forbid some types of financial instruments or custom may discourage them. In many Latin American countries, for instance, legal codes may not permit the use of convertible debentures; in some, they are permitted but simply not used.

There is a widespread conviction that a development bank ought to revolve its funds as rapidly as possible, selling not only its portfolio of securities but also its subsidiary enterprises as soon as it can do so advantageously. By turning over its resources more quickly, the bank recovers its funds for reinvestment in other enterprises. In this way it can increase the amount of private investment in industry and stimulate the circulation of private securities. Selling out, however, involves difficulties in addition to those already mentioned, even assuming it is possible to find a buyer. The development bank will be able to sell only its sound and profitable investments. It may be forced to hold on to the failures, thus adversely affecting its own profitability, impairing its reputation, reducing its ability to sell its own securities and complicating its management problems. Moreover, in some cases, an effort to sell after a long period of inflation might expose a development bank to a large capital gains tax, with the result that no sale will be made.

At first blush, it might appear that a privately-owned, profit-directed development bank would take a different view of selling out its investments or enterprises than would a government-owned institution. The private institution, it may be thought, with its eye on profits, might be tempted to hold on to precisely those securities which it could most readily sell. In fact, however, it may be less interested in steady, sure income than in taking a substantial capital gain and using the proceeds to do the same again, taking into account, of course, its portfolio as a whole. It certainly will sell the moment there is a more profitable use for its capital. On the other hand, a government development bank is likely to find itself under severe pressure from both the public and the parliament when it tries to sell profitable enterprises and may be sorely tempted and pressed to maintain foundering enterprises with the proceeds of profitable ones. As a result, few government development banks sell out their enterprises completely. Thus the Nacional Financiera, despite its announced policy, has sold few of the enterprises it set up. The Puerto Rico Industrial Development Company is reluctant to part with the profitable Caribe Hilton Hotel, although it has said it would do so (at a price).

Still, despite the difficulties and temptations, development banks sometimes sell out if they are determined to do so. The Puerto Rico Industrial Development Company sold all its industrial plants to a private buyer in 1950. But the more typical practice has been a partial rather than a complete sale of equity, with the result that jointly owned companies have emerged and that, while the development bank retains an interest, sometimes controlling, securities of the company begin to circulate. The Industrial Development Corporation of Pakistan limits the number of shares of its enterprises that may be sold to any one individual, so as to prevent control by a single person or group, and thereby diffuses ownership of industrial securities.

The provision of capital and initiative is not always sufficient to create effective enterprise. Entrepreneurs may need technical advice on the preparation of projects and on their execution and management. Many development banks find that a substantial number of the entrepreneurs who come to them have neither the technical nor the organizational experience to work out a project. The reply to an application for financing in underdeveloped countries, and not only there, can rarely be a simple yes or no. The reply must take the form of a discussion of the applicant's proposal and methods of financing, constructing and operating the project. Where the project is of any substantial size, both the project and its proposed financing may change in the course of discussion, to the mutual benefit of both applicant and development bank. Nor does the need for technical advice end with the working out of a project and provision of finance; technical guidance may have to continue over the life of the investment, as new problems and difficulties emerge. The development bank must therefore have a technical and advisory staff, and this need involves a bank in heavy expense as well as in the difficulties of finding qualified personnel.

The task and the expense will be the greater if the institution undertakes or sponsors surveys to look for or to mark out profitable fields of investment. In this latter field, such institutions as the Chilean Corporación de Fomento and the Mexican Nacional Financiera have been prominent. They have built up large technical and economic research staffs, which have not only served directly the purposes of the institution, but have also provided a training ground for technicians for the country in general. The Turkish Industrial Development Bank has only rarely ventured into the field of industrial surveys (and then only to deal with special problems), largely because of the expense involved. It has limited itself to giving technical advice to its clients by studying their projects carefully, showing them the technical and administrative pitfalls and providing them with financial and technical help in the course of end-use investigations throughout the life of a loan. The Industrial Development Corporation of South Africa, on the other hand, conducts research and experimental work and carries out resource surveys, sometimes at the request of the Government.

The activities cited so far are by no means a complete list of the aids to industry that development banks give or could give. For instance, a large part of the activity of the American local and regional development banks consists of building factories or launching industrial estates, for sale or lease (usually with an option to buy) to industry. This has also become the main activity of the Puerto Rico Industrial Development Company. By the end of 1954, about 78 per cent of its investments in industries consisted of land and buildings (and some equipment) on rental to industrial firms. Sometimes, as in the case of the Caribe Hilton Hotel, the lease is made on a profit-sharing basis. The Company also assists private industrialists in their negotiations with the Commonwealth Government on tax exemption, etc., and cooperates with its Education Department in the setting up of training programs of use to industry. The Industrial Development Bank of Turkey does some normal commercial business with its borrowers. In this, it follows the lead of similar institutions in advanced countries, both in the nineteenth century and now, but it also runs the risk of alienating the commercial banks which are its main shareholders. Some banks, like the Pakistan Industrial Finance Corporation, are authorized to accept deposits. The Industrial Development Bank of Turkey may also do so, but has denied itself this privilege in order to qualify for the greater privilege of a special parliamentary exemption from the national banking law. Some development banks sponsor training programs. The Chilean Corporación de Fomento has carried its educational activity to the point of sponsoring fellowships abroad for particular types of technical training. Finally, a development bank can contribute to development by the effect of demonstration and can call particular needs to the attention of the government.

In this long and incomplete list of activities, the provision of initiative and of technical assistance in the creation and management of new enterprises may well be the most important. Achievement of these objectives is an important contribution indeed. But the hard core of a development bank's activities is financing those enterprises. And here it clearly treads on risky ground. Its lending is medium- and long-term. Its participations are made in new enterprises in untried fields. Its investments may yield no returns for a long time, though its overhead will be high from the start. There will be little possibility, in most underdeveloped countries, of selling securities from its portfolio. If the bank has to borrow its funds and concentrate on lending, the margins on which it will operate must obviously be very small. The prospects are brighter if other types of investment are made, but the risks are inherently greater. The risks can of course be minimized or even eliminated, simply by making no investments at all. But venture is what is required in the private sector, and the development bank has presumably been set up precisely to take these risks. The trick is to strike the fine line between excess of caution and excess of zeal. Special attention must be given to the method of financing the development bank and special care must be taken in the selection of its management. Financing must pay due regard to the risks and illiquidity of the bank's investments. Management must have a rare combination of good judgment and imagination, and concern for management must not be limited to the development bank itself, but must extend to its clients as well.

Financing the Bank

How large should a development bank's resources be and where should they come from? Both the size and origin of its resources have a direct bearing on its purpose and activities, and vice versa.

The risk implicit in a development bank's operations and the likelihood of an initial period with little earnings and probably no profits suggest the desirability of getting as much equity as possible in relation to loan capital. On the other hand, a higher proportion of loan capital, though it may impose heavy fixed charges, improves the earning power of the equity invested in the bank. The importance of earning power will be very great if the equity comes from private sources, which will expect dividends. It may be of little significance if all the resources come from the government. But in either event, the uncertainties inherent in long-term financing in new fields require a considerable proportion of risk capital.

What is a reasonable ratio of debt to equity? There can be no precise or sure answer to this question, though it is obviously affected by the degree to which the development bank proposes to divide its investments between equity and loans. The debt-equity ratios of development banks actually in operation vary widely. The Industrial Bank of Japan was able to borrow up to 10 times its capital. The Industrial Finance Corporation of India may borrow up to five times its equity and reserves. The Turkish Industrial Development Bank has no statutory limit on its borrowings, and special legislation exempts it from the severe restrictions on borrowing imposed by the Turkish Commercial Code. Nevertheless, its borrowing is narrowly limited by the provisions of its loan contracts with the World Bank. In helping set up and finance development banks, the World Bank has insisted on an initial debt-equity ratio no greater than three to one, increasing it only in the light of experience.

Where should the capital come from? It may be taken for granted that a large fraction will come from the government, directly or indirectly. Indeed, the initiative in the creation of a development bank is likely to come from the government, as part of a policy to stimulate private investment. And the effect of that stimulus is likely to be directly related to the amount of funds the government provides, since these may be cheap funds, available at less than the going cost of capital. Should the government then provide all the capital of the new bank?

If an increase in the amount of capital available for long-term investment is indeed a matter of concern, an effort will be made to get private capital into the institution. The resources of the government or of public agencies will be drawn on only to make up the difference between what can be obtained from private sources and the amount considered necessary for a viable and effective institution. There are other good reasons for minimizing the governmental contribution. Generally governments have difficulty enough in mobilizing the resources required to finance the investments that they alone can make; and the demand for such investment is often so great that part of it must be forgone or postponed unless governments fall back on deficit financing to a degree likely to result in inflation. Moreover, the independence of the management of the institution from pressures both private and bureaucratic may be strengthened by the extent to which its ownership is diffused. This last is a consideration to which governments as well as private shareholders, both concerned with sound and honest operations, will probably give much weight.

Attracting private capital for a new investment institution is not likely to be easy, else there might be no need for a government to take the initiative in creating the institution. But the government can offer many inducements, such as a guaranteed minimum dividend or tax-free dividends. Bonds of the institution can be given various privileges and immunities, and the government can grant subsidies which considerably enhance earning power while earning no return of their own. The experience of the World Bank in Turkey and in India suggests that a serious effort can bring in investors who were initially reluctant and that the promise of high profits is not the only attraction for certain classes of shareholders. And the experience of Turkey further suggests that a bank with an initially narrow range of shareholders can considerably extend their number, once it has become well-known and has given evidence of its competence and earning capacity. (The Industrial Development Bank of Turkey now has more than 400 shareholders, compared to the original 18, and its shares sell at around 140.) This is not to say that private equity will always be available; there was none in Ethiopia when its Development Bank was set up, and there was no alternative to the use of government capital for the bank's entire requirements. In some cases where private equity was not forthcoming, governments have more or less unabashedly applied pressures to various institutions to take up shares or bonds of a development bank. Such action, however undesirable, has fundamentally the same justification as using government funds for the bank's capital. In each case the government acts as a mobilizer of resources which, on their return to the private sector, will be used in a different and presumably better way.

But under the right conditions and with appropriate inducements, some private capital is likely to be forthcoming, chiefly from banks and other financial institutions which provide a large part of the equity of most development banks. It is equally likely in many cases that the amount thus brought together will not be large enough to permit the institution to get started effectively. Assistance from the government, the central bank or other government institutions is then essential. The provision of such resources may, indeed, help to bring forth more private capital than would otherwise have been possible.

Government finance can take the form of voting or non-voting shares or loans. Which it is to be depends primarily on the government's decision on its role in the management of the institution and what effect that decision is likely to have on the private sector. Government participation in common stock immediately involves it in direction; participation in preferred shares or financing by loans would not necessarily do so.

Various devices may be used to make government capital available in a form which does not require voting participation or control. In Japan the Treasury deposited large sums with the Industrial Bank, on a permanent basis. In India and Ceylon, where all the equity in the new development banks is privately owned, the governments have made 30-year interest-free loans; in the event of liquidation, the banks need to repay the loans only after all other creditors have been repaid and shareholders have recovered their investment. Such interest-free loans can provide a tremendous leverage for earnings on equity, which cannot but be attractive to shareholders. In Turkey, the Industrial Development Bank, also privately owned, obtained the right to borrow from the Central Bank at a low rate and, more important, was made the agent for the lending of Marshall Plan counterpart funds, at an agreed commission.[10] The method used in India provides an extra advantage in that the funds were made available at the very start and hence, invested in short-term securities, yield a return which subsidizes the bank until it can build up its long-term investments. In Turkey's case, the agency contract covering use of funds also provided immediate and assured income with no risk of loss to the Industrial Development Bank.

The magnitude and form of the government contribution obviously affect the rate of interest which the institution will have to charge on its loans and the terms and conditions on which it will make other investments. Since government loans can be made at an arbitrary rate of interest or entirely interest-free or can be provided on an equity basis with no need for dividends, they can play an important part in keeping re-lending rates at reasonable levels until the volume of operations builds up or in stimulating venturesome investments. The government contribution is thus of particular importance in the first stage of a development bank's operations. Its importance thereafter may be simply a question of the degree of subsidy, if any, a government wishes to continue to provide.

In financing a development bank, in whatever form, a government will be guided by the same considerations and criteria that affect its outlays for other purposes. That is, it will need to consider the effect of its fiscal and financial operations on the economy. This it

---

[10] U. S. counterpart funds have also been used to help finance the Development Bank of Japan. In the Philippines, the proceeds of sale of U. S. surplus property provided two-thirds of the capital of the Rehabilitation Finance Corporation. Other techniques are used elsewhere for making counterpart funds available for private enterprise.

can most appropriately do by providing funds through the regular budgetary process, so that the significance of financing the development bank can be clearly seen and assessed. The financing of the budget may in fact require borrowing from the central bank, but the fact that it does is consciously noted, its effect measured and the step deliberately taken. Direct financing by the central bank, particularly on a continuing basis through lending or re-discounting, is too easily open to abuse. The central bank ought to be in a position to deal with the development bank as it does with the rest of the banking system, in the light of the requirements of monetary policy.[11]

When a development bank is responsible for making general economic surveys or providing general services to industry in addition to those incident to its conventional tasks and investments, these costs ought not to be covered from its capital or income. In fact, can a small development bank hope, itself, to cover such expenses? Here is a reasonably clear case for a government contribution. It can, of course, be argued that in a government-owned bank it makes no difference whether, for instance, research and survey costs come out of income, thus reducing profit to the government, or from special appropriations. There is merit, however, in distinguishing types of functions, in terms perhaps of the incidence of preponderant benefit. The distinction can be important in measuring the viability of the institution, which will affect its reputation and credit standing. This is the kind of distinction made in the Ordinance which created the Uganda Development Corporation. There the Government is specifically authorized to pay for or to contribute towards the cost of any research or research institute which, aside from benefiting the Corporation, "is of benefit to the Protectorate as a whole."

---

[11] This is not to say that a central bank should never share in the financing of a development bank. There may be good reason for it to provide part or all of the original finance required. Thus in Canada, the Industrial Development Bank was incorporated as a subsidiary of the Bank of Canada. In England and in India, the ICFC and the IFC were set up with a specified amount of share capital from the Bank of England and the Reserve Bank of India, respectively. In Turkey, loans from the Central Bank were arranged at the time the Industrial Development Bank was set up, but the sum involved was clearly specified in advance. What is important is that, except for clearly specified sums, the central bank should not lose control over what could become an important part of its operations.

In Ethiopia, the management of the Development Bank wished in the first year to make general surveys of certain fields in search of investment opportunities, felt the expense was too great to be carried by the Bank, and was unable to obtain grants for research and educational purposes from the Government or from other institutions. In India, the method by which the Government has helped finance the ICICI provides a subsidy which could be used for such purposes. In Ceylon and Burma, special research institutions have been set up to provide technical advice and assistance to various types of entrepreneurs, thus relieving the development banks in those countries of a part of the burden. In Puerto Rico, responsibility for some of the planning, research and promotion was transferred from the Industrial Development Company to the Economic Development Administration, a government department of which the Company is a subsidiary. In an inverse way, this distinction is made in the Industrial Development Corporation of Pakistan, whose small government-provided capital is intended primarily to finance research and surveys, but whose large investments are financed by special ad hoc appropriations.

Some financial institutions have managed to obtain foreign capital, sometimes equity but more often loans. Indeed, in some Latin American countries, development banks were created so that foreign governments would have a more or less public institution through which to make loans for specific projects. Thus, the Export-Import Bank provided most of the capital of the Bolivian Corporación de Fomento which was created to make pre-agreed use of those funds, and the Nacional Financiera of Mexico and the Development Bank of Japan have been intermediaries for certain World Bank loans. On the private side, although on a more modest basis, private foreign equity contributed substantially to the Japanese Industrial Bank earlier in the century, as it has today to the ICICI. The participation of foreign capital, in whatever form, is important in countries which are short of foreign exchange. But it makes an even more important contribution through the skills and experience which will accompany it, especially if the foreign capital participates directly, and through the confidence it will give to other investors, foreign and domestic. Of course, except that the government is more likely to provide guarantees and leverage for a development bank than for an ordinary enterprise, it will be no easier to attract foreign capital for a development bank than for any other purpose. Whether or not such capital is forthcoming will depend on those same factors of "climate" and profitability that affect foreign investment generally.

Among the present sources of foreign capital is the World Bank, which has helped to set up several development banks and has granted lines of credit to three of them. A loan from the World Bank, as from any foreign lender who insists on repayment in foreign currency, raises the question of the exchange risk. If the currency of the borrower is devalued, it becomes more expensive to buy the foreign exchange required to repay the World Bank. Who should take this risk of devaluation? The development bank, which could be wiped out as a result of a devaluation early in its career? A borrower who uses his loan in an export industry might be able to offset the losses of devaluation, but few borrowers in underdeveloped countries are likely to be engaged in producing for export. Should then the ultimate borrower take the risk of impairing his capital or perhaps of bankruptcy? Or should the risk be taken by the government, even though this would amount to subsidizing certain enterprises (those which borrow foreign currency from the development bank) but not others?

In Ethiopia, no such problem arose, for the Government (not the Development Bank) was the borrower from the World Bank and assumed the exchange risk automatically. In Ceylon, the Government has agreed to accept the exchange risk of a loan to the Development Finance Corporation from the World Bank up to a specified amount, though no loan has yet been made. In Turkey, the Government refused to accept the risk at the time the loan was negotiated and borrowers would not do so unless their loans were to finance purchases of equipment which could be obtained only in the United States. For with Turkey's adherence to the European Payments Union in 1950, the Turkish authorities made European currencies freely available for capital goods imports and it was from Europe that most of the capital goods required by Turkish industries came. Thus it was obviously advantageous to borrow Turkish liras from the Industrial Development Bank and convert them into foreign exchange at the Central Bank, rather than to borrow foreign exchange and run the risk of devaluation—unless there was no choice, which was the case only when United States currency, in very short supply, was involved. As a result, the proceeds of the World Bank's loan remained virtually unused, and the Industrial Development Bank's domestic currency resources became rapidly committed. The growing stringency of Turkey's foreign exchange position and the threatened slowdown of the Industrial Development Bank's operations led to a resolution of the problem in early 1953, when the Central Bank in effect assumed the risk of devaluation, for a small fee which the Industrial Development Bank passed on to its borrowers.[12] This was a complete solution. In Mexico, the Bank of Mexico agreed for a small fee to assume the risk on only half the loans granted by the short-lived consortium to which the World Bank had made a loan. This compromise had little attraction. In India, where the World Bank's loan still remains unused, foreign exchange has recently become very tight, with the result that the ICICI's borrowers are expected to become willing to assume the risk.

The experience of the World Bank with respect to the exchange risk issue points up the importance of making foreign loans available in a manner which will not create a bias towards leaving them unused and drawing heavily on domestic currency resources either until the latter are exhausted or until a severe shortage of foreign exchange provokes governmental restrictions on its allocation. Unless the expenditure programs of a government are sufficiently large to exhaust foreign exchange resources, exchange authorities are likely to continue making exchange available for private imports of capital

---

[12] This solution does not end the foreign exchange risk issue unless the maturities of the Industrial Development Bank's loans correspond precisely with those of the World Bank loan. This is not likely to be the case; the former will generally be shorter than the latter. At the moment of repayment, therefore, the risk reverts to the Development Bank. The Turkish Government, at first unwilling to protect the individual entrepreneur, was from the start prepared to protect the Development Bank. Accordingly, it agreed to convert into foreign exchange the Turkish lira payments of principal, interest and other income from the Bank's investments in foreign exchange. The Development Bank thus had foreign exchange available, which it could use to repay or prepay the World Bank or for additional investments. In this manner, the Development Bank was protected and at the same time acquired a revolving fund of foreign exchange resources. As of the end of 1956, the Development Bank had reinvested $1.19 million from this source.

goods. The bias is then likely to continue until a development bank has left only its foreign exchange resources, an event which would restrict its operations unless it or its borrowers decided to assume the exchange risk.

Most development banks are empowered to borrow from private sources at home, but unfortunately, in many countries bonds are difficult to sell. The investing public usually insists upon confidence, profits and liquidity, and these are not always available. Nor will a treasury guarantee help if the value of money is declining. In Turkey's inflationary situation, no one will buy bonds if he can help it and the Industrial Development Bank has been unable to float a public bond issue. The Chilean Fomento has been equally powerless for the same reason (even though it is a government corporation and its bonds would carry a government guarantee). Moreover, without a securities market, there can be little liquidity and until a development bank is well established it cannot instill confidence. Perhaps the most notable success in the issuance of development bank bonds has been the participation certificates of the Mexican Financiera, but that success has been based on complete liquidity and official backing. The Industrial Finance Corporation of India has more than doubled its resources by the sale of bonds and debentures; these, too, rest on government guarantees. The comparable institution in Pakistan has had much more difficulty, due partly (but not entirely) to inflationary pressures.

In short, while some development banks have been successful in raising funds in domestic bond markets, the success of many has undoubtedly depended either on their official position or on official support. And in an inflationary situation, neither is likely to be sufficient, even though that situation might well bring forth a greater demand for financing from the development bank.

The risks involved in its investments, the difficulties of mobilizing the requisite capital and the desirability of getting as much private capital as possible suggest that particular attention be addressed to the following points concerning capitalization of a development bank:

(1) A development bank must start from a strong financial position. Its resources must not only be sufficient to meet a large overhead and continuing calls for finance, but they must be

balanced between sufficient equity to take risks and to stand possible losses and enough debt to assure a return attractive to equity. How large the total capital should be depends on circumstances. But it must clearly be large enough to permit the institution to do its job effectively over a reasonable period. The bank cannot start on a shoe-string.

(2) A main activity of a development bank is to provide enterprises with capital on reasonable terms. Those terms must be related to the manner in which and cost at which the institution obtains its own resources. Rates on loans granted must bear some relationship to the cost of borrowing and the risk of lending. The volume of equity investments must be related to the equity invested in the development bank itself (or to other resources on which the institution bears no risk). The "mix" of the bank's investments has a bearing on the volume and conditions of each type of investment and is related to the sources and cost of the development bank's resources. Special privileges granted by the government can help to lower the cost of obtaining private capital, though such privileges are a subsidy to the shareholders or to the development bank.

(3) A development bank financed entirely by government capital could offer the cheapest funds, but government capital provided at less than cost constitutes an additional subsidy. More important, there are compelling reasons for minimizing the governmental contribution in relation to the funds obtained from the private sector.

(4) The method of providing capital to the bank's clients must also be related to the circumstances of the client and the country. Flexibility is vital and should be subject to no limitations other than the requirements of law and the inhibitions of custom.

Thus the management of the bank must be capable of dealing with various types of resources and of balancing the burdens imposed by the bank's capital structure with the conditions of the bank's investments. Considerations of diversification of investments and limitations on the size of any single investment (in relation to the bank's capital) need to be taken into account here.

The Bank's Relationship to the Government

When a government sponsors a development bank to stimulate the private sector, it must decide on the role it will play in its direction and management. Since the government sets up the bank to facilitate the execution of a particular policy or program and particularly since it contributes (usually to a great extent) to the finances of the institution, it is futile to expect the government to stand aside completely and permit the "independence" that a private corporation enjoys. Its concern is multiple in that it is interested in increasing investment, in channelling that investment in particular directions and in assuring the proper use of public funds.

Where all or a majority of the equity has been provided by the government, the latter has the right, as would any majority stockholder, to participate in the direction of the bank. Its participation may take the form simply of laying down broad policies on investment priorities, or of appointing all or part of the board of directors with all that that implies with regard to decision-making, or of direct control over management. Given the climate of opinion in the underdeveloped countries, it is likely that the right somehow to participate in policy will be exercised. The issue becomes more acute when all or most of the equity is provided by private individuals or institutions. In such cases, the government's right to participate in direction will be limited, but it will be no less concerned with making its influence felt and with assuring itself that the funds it has provided are being used honestly and well.

Government participation in the direction of development banks varies widely and usually reflects the composition of the share capital of the banks concerned. In the new Development Finance Corporation of Ceylon, whose equity comes from private sources, the shareholders select the board (after the retirement of the initial members), except that as long as any part of a loan from the Government is outstanding the Finance Minister has the right to appoint a director. A similar situation prevails in India's ICICI. In Turkey, although the Industrial Development Bank is also private, the Central Bank has a direct voice in the selection of one member of the board (who must, however, be a stockholder), in consideration of its loans to the Bank. The Japanese Government, which provides all of the equity of the

Japanese Development Bank, also appoints all its directors. In Mexico, the Government shares with the minority (private) stockholders of the Nacional Financiera the right to appoint the board. In Puerto Rico, the government-owned Industrial Development Company no longer has a board of directors; it has been made a subsidiary of the Economic Development Administration, whose administrator takes the place of the directors of the Company. In general, the managers of these institutions are appointed by their boards of directors, although appointment by governments, upon or without the nominations of the boards, is not uncommon.

Where a development bank is government-owned and clearly and overtly an instrument of government policy to be coordinated with other instruments, there are some advantages to be gained by not having a board of directors, as in the case of the Puerto Rican institution. Still, a board can be a very useful screen and protection for management, which might be seriously hampered if it were directly responsible to a government official.

The important issue in the bank's relations to the government does not, however, concern the appointment of the board of directors and the manager. It concerns rather the powers and quality of the management. A government setting up a development bank, with or without subscribing to its equity and with or without the right to appoint members of the board, will wish to keep the bank's management as free as possible from the inevitable pressures that will be applied by both political and private vested business interests. It is in order thus to insulate the management from shifts in political power and from political interests that the World Bank has urged that, wherever possible, all voting stock be held in private hands and, in order to protect the management from special private interests, that the stock be as widely dispersed as possible. But neither the one nor the other of these is always practicable.

Thus the issue facing the government is fundamentally the same as the one it faces in its relations with any of its corporate or autonomous entities. How can the operating flexibility and independence required for the successful operation of an enterprise be reconciled with the need for controls to assure public accountability for the use of public funds and to assure consistency with public policy? The need for such independence and flexibility is greater in a bank or investment institution than in the normal enterprise because of the unusually heavy reliance on personal, experienced judgment. The way out of this dilemma is not usually found in statutory provisions. Indeed, as long as any government capital is involved (and sometimes even if there is none), no statutory provision will prevent the government from participating or interfering in the bank's management if it is determined to do so. Thus in the case of the Industrial Development Bank, the Turkish Government had no rights with respect to the board and the Central Bank had the right to participate in the selection of only one director out of seven; but the Government once forced the board to resign and twice put up to the stockholders new slates of board members, which were promptly elected with no articulate protest from the stockholders.

The right line between independence and responsibility is more likely to be found in satisfactory working relationships, worked out by judicious practice and experiment. These are more apt to be achieved when the management is strong and competent and the government restrained and when there is a free exchange of information and views among the bank, the administration, the parliament and the public. Such a situation will help the bank to create the kind of cooperation and sympathetic goodwill it needs to maintain its independence, without ever completely freeing it from criticism and the danger of pressure. On the other hand, the kind of government participation in direction which reserves to the government the power of decision with regard to each investment lays the bank open to favoritism, whim and over-optimism, and deprives the management of the flexibility it needs. And a development bank management which remains unaware of government development policy will quickly find its wings clipped.

Not all governments are prepared to remain in the background, relying on consultation and mutual understanding and perhaps a statement of priorities, but leaving decisions to the boards and management which they are instrumental in appointing and which they are normally in a position to remove. Power of decision often rests with the government when development banks are directly authorized to take the initiative in specific industries and projects which the government feels are not receiving sufficient investment. The Government of Pakistan has laid out the several fields of activity to which the Industrial Development Corporation should direct its attention. It requires the Corporation to submit each of its investment projects in those fields for individual approval. Separate budgetary allocations are required to finance each one approved. The South African Industrial Development Corporation is in practice under a similar restriction when it decides to create a subsidiary for which it needs additions to its capital. The National Industrial Development Corporation of India receives specific assignments laid down in the Five-Year Plan and allocations of funds accordingly. Such cases as these involve development banks normally dealing with very large projects, for which the initiative lies with the development banks or the governments. But that kind of government participation may also occur in development banks dealing with relatively small investments in loan form. If the Indonesian State Bank for Industry refuses to grant a loan "because such financing may be unjustifiable from a banking point of view or because it does not fall within its competency," the Finance Minister may instruct it to do so.[13] (He may also, if requested, guarantee the Bank against losses or illiquidity from such loans.) On the other hand, the statutes of the development banks of Turkey and Ceylon contain no provision requiring approval by or association with the government in investment decisions; yet the presence of a government representative or spokesman on the board and the good sense of the management are likely to assure the required mutual understanding of objectives and decisions.

These various relationships between governments and development banks illustrate the ways in which a development bank is fitted into an "economic plan." Such a bank, if a government does sponsor and support it, comes into existence as part of a national program or plan, however vague. What is the connection between the bank and the program? There are few examples to look at, because of the paucity of comprehensive programs. Among the few are the Puerto Rico Industrial Development Company, which was set up as part of a plan for development of the Island, and India's National Industrial

---

[13] *Bank Industri Negara 1951-1956* (Djakarta, 1956), p. 81.

Development Corporation, which has an assigned task in the Second Five-Year Plan.

A development program normally consists of two separate but closely related parts. There is a program of government expenditures, consisting chiefly of capital outlays, and there is a group of policies to stimulate productive activity in the private sector. The targets of the former, assuming they have been soundly set, are more or less under control of the government, for they are assignments to the departments of government. The targets of the latter are hopeful estimates of the ways in which the private sector, and the entrepreneurial community in particular, will respond to the policies and activities of the government. Obviously, the government's own targets are also affected by private responses. The interrelation of the programs is too close to permit separation.

The activity of a development bank as conceived here—a stimulant to the private sector—belongs in the private sector. Its role is to help produce the desired response by providing capital, initiative and technical advice. Within this general framework, there is room for wide variation in methods of working. While the ICICI is expected by the Indian authorities to make a contribution to the achievement of the Five-Year Plan, its activities can only be estimated. The Indian Government has helped to provide its capital and can now do no more than add the ICICI's resources to those of other sources of finance in estimating whether there will be sufficient finance for the investment the private sector is hopefully expected to undertake in the next five years. This relationship, which may seem tenuous, is by no means unimportant nor does it stand alone. In the first place, the development bank has been set up to provide the missing ingredients of investment, and the presumption is that something will happen, that is, that the private sector will respond, if these ingredients become available. In the second place, the government is presumably pursuing other policies both to push and to lure entrepreneurs into productive investment. The combination of a development bank and effective policies can be very influential.

The relationship between a development bank and a development program can be even closer. The Marshall Plan Private Enterprise Fund administered by the Industrial Development Bank of Turkey can be used only for investment in a specified group of industries, in order of priority determined by the Turkish and American Governments. This priority list is intended to reflect the nation's most urgent industrial needs. The Development Bank's use of the Fund is thus in accordance with some general conception of what Turkey requires, although the specific investment decisions remain the responsibility of the Development Bank. So in Pakistan, the Industrial Development Corporation is governed by a specific priority list drawn by the Government.

A step further along the way is the case of the Puerto Rican institution, where the head of a government department takes the place of a board of directors and where the programs are governed by budgetary allocations and decisions. Here the government budget is a "marching order" and an instrument of coordination for the Company no less than for the regular administrative departments, although each individual decision appears to rest with the Company. In India, the National Industrial Development Corporation is even more fully integrated into the Government's program. The Corporation is intended to take up specific projects laid out in the Plan, for which it receives specific allocations of funds. The Corporation, having worked out the project in close association with government departments, will presumably seek private participation in financing them. If such participation is not forthcoming, it will proceed on its own in order to help achieve the targets of the Plan. Only experience will tell whether this kind of relationship will leave any initiative or decision to the Corporation, whether the Corporation can in any sense be considered a part of the private sector, and whether it is not in fact only an administrative device for handling government investments.

These are not the only ways of achieving coordination between development banks which are instruments of governmental policy and other government bodies and programs. There are other devices as well. But whatever method is used, it is important that it should not be one which will stifle the initiative and independence of judgment which the institution should have if it is to help to stimulate the private sector of the economy. Dependence on the government for investment-by-investment allocations of funds or for periodic contributions for which a government decision must be made each time or for approval of individual investments can limit the flexibility and independence of decision that a development bank needs.

The Bank's Relationship to the Enterprises It Finances

A development bank which finances enterprises, whether by loan or equity and whether in participation with others or alone, faces the issue of its relationship to those enterprises. If a bank lends on security, which is the most likely case, it might take little interest in the operations of its borrower and limit itself to the collection of service payments. This would not, however, be a wise course, because the security may not be marketable and because the development bank will presumably be concerned as much with the effectiveness of its loan as with its repayment. It can demonstrate that concern best by close supervision of the loan and, perhaps, by membership on the board of the borrower.

The ICICI, when it makes a loan, requires regular reports from its borrowers, covering technical and financial aspects of the loan and the firm; in this connection it sometimes requires changes in accounting methods. It also insists on the right to make regular inspections of the project and the firm and to appoint a director; it does not, however, always exercise the latter right, for it seeks as far as possible to avoid any responsibility for the management of its clients. The Turkish Industrial Development Bank has similar requirements and stresses regular reporting by the borrower and regular inspections by its own engineers and accountants. It seeks to appraise the management of the enterprise and offers technical and financial advice whenever it seems appropriate. The Turkish bank has not found this process an easy one, for the business community, accustomed to minding its own business, is not yet reconciled to the fact that the business of a bank is its client's business; and even bankers do not know much about the enterprises they finance. Unwillingness to let the Industrial Development Bank learn the details of their operations has influenced some potential borrowers to withdraw their applications. While this situation has not led the Industrial Development Bank to relax its information and inspection requirements, it has persuaded it not to insist upon board membership.

Many development banks appear to follow this principle of close continuing contact with their borrowers, while exhibiting the same reluctance to take part in direction of the firm. The purpose, of course, is to assure effective use of the loan and to be in a position to detect difficulties in the project or the firm as early as possible so that advice and assistance, if accepted, may not come too late.

The problem is more acute when a development bank holds equity in a firm, with the voting rights and board membership that may go along with equity. Reluctance to share equity severely limits a development bank's activity in such countries as Turkey. Most development banks do take board membership in the case of participations and, of course, have no means of avoiding the responsibility of direction in the case of a full-fledged subsidiary. Still, the reluctance to accept responsibility is so strong in the Turkish Industrial Development Bank that only when its equity is more than 50 per cent of the stock does it insist on a majority on the board and when its equity is less than 15 per cent it does not ask for any representation at all.

In the advanced countries large-scale bank participation in the financing of enterprises has usually gone hand-in-hand with bank participation in their direction and, in the earlier years especially, that close association became an important conduit for technical advice and financial accommodation. Given the prevailing lack of managerial experience, there are advantages to using the management and staff of the development bank as a pool of skills and experience available to its clients. But there are obvious dangers too: the bank may become a powerful director of a large segment of the nation's industry; the institution's personnel may be spread so thinly over many enterprises as to make it difficult for it to do its job effectively; the client's management may not be allowed the authority it must have if it is to direct the enterprise effectively; good money may be thrown after bad if things go wrong with the firm; and there may be a tendency not to finance competitive enterprise.

It is probably desirable to limit the institution's relations to its clients to making sure that the management is satisfactory and to offering technical advice and policy guidance where necessary, while remaining clear of operational responsibility. Board membership can be an effective channel for such policy guidance, for it not only gives the bank a forum for its views and advice but may also facilitate the sale of its shares by giving confidence to prospective buyers. In this manner, too, the bank can play an important role in stimulating the growth of managerial experience. But the bank will wish to consider carefully the distinction between advice and participation in policy, on the one hand, and direct management on the other. In Mexico, the Nacional Financiera has investments in almost 200 enterprises, in many cases large enough to make the enterprise qualify as a "subsidiary." Each of these enterprises is governed by its own board of directors, with (sometimes) a representative of the Nacional Financiera as a member and a member of the technical department assigned as an adviser or chief engineer of the enterprise.

Personnel Requirements of the Bank

Everything that has been said so far about a development bank—its purpose, its financing, its policies—emphasizes the need for competent, experienced personnel. Running a development bank is not a routine job. It requires skill, judgment and imagination, as well as a proper concern for other people's or the government's money.

Most development banks are run along the lines of a firm with a board of directors, a general manager or managing director, and a technical staff. In some respects, the board of directors is the easiest group to find; for there is no country in which some men of experience and wisdom capable of laying down broad policy are not to be found. Aside from its policy-making function, a board has two other functions of importance. It can use its influence to support and further the interests of the bank and to help to insulate the management of the bank from the pressures, both public and private, which will inevitably be brought to bear on it. The latter is a function which some managers of banks welcome, although it may not always be welcome to board members.

When governments create development banks and appoint their board members, they have the opportunity to call on the nation's ablest people. Yet they often limit their choice to their own officials and civil servants and sometimes to members of parliament. Sometimes a board of cabinet members or members of parliament transfers to the board meetings political struggles better left elsewhere. At best, a board limited to such persons does not enjoy the breadth of experience possible when its members are chosen from a variety of fields. Private shareholders are similarly prone to choose board members from their own ranks. In Turkey, the Industrial Development Bank's stockholders, who have the power to select board members, and the government, which has helped to exercise that power, have both been singularly free of this kind of self-interested provincialism; its boards have been broadly based, with members drawn from commerce, industry, law, banking and the universities, not from government, and with a view apparently to tapping useful experience rather than to direct representation of interests. The National Industrial Development Corporation of India has similarly sought breadth of experience.

More difficult than the selection of a board is the selection of top executives, who almost by definition are in short supply in underdeveloped countries. The manager of a development bank, particularly one which is new and laboring under great difficulties, should have a combination of skills that would be rare anywhere. It is not unlikely that many countries, for a time at least, will have to seek their managers and perhaps executive officers abroad. If so, additional qualities of understanding and adaptability are required, for it is very easy to take for granted in an underdeveloped country the circumstances and attitudes now normal in advanced countries. The problem is to find an executive staff capable of carrying out a full delegation of authority from the board of directors, not for the establishment of basic policies, but for operational management, and to find competent technicians to attach to the executive officers.

Wherever the manager comes from, he must be granted sufficient authority, under basic policies, to do his job: to engage and dismiss personnel and make all daily decisions. The only legitimate limitation on the authority of a competent manager is the board's right to set general policy, to approve or reject his investment recommendations and to replace him if it is not satisfied with his work. In some development banks, boards have gone further and have delegated to their managers the final decisions on some kinds of loans of limited amounts. Needless to say, to leave the operational responsibility in the hands of a manager requires that he have the full confidence of the board, so that it is prepared to accept his statements at face value without inquiring into every detail of administration. That kind of delegation can work only where the manager is experienced and competent. It is not likely to work where his appointment has been due to nepotism or political favor, unless of course he happens to be qualified on his merits.

Much the same may be said of the technical staff of a development bank, some of whom may also have to come from abroad. A development bank, if it is to do its work adequately, needs accountants, engineers, financial analysts, economists and that variety of person whose experience has sharpened his ability to judge by intuition the creditworthiness of a potential borrower or the value of a prospective investment. Such personnel must be capable both of judging the merits of a proposal and of advising how it can be improved and how enterprises can be strengthened. The problem of finding such personnel is aggravated to the extent that the development bank undertakes responsibility for direction or management of the enterprises it finances. In developed countries, investment institutions can often rely on the existence of a large pool of technicians on whom they can draw for consultation when necessary. Such a pool is rarely available in underdeveloped countries, and a development bank usually has to keep on its payroll most of the staff it needs.

Good managers are expensive. They are not in plentiful supply and are in great demand everywhere. The same is true to an only slightly lesser extent of other executive and technical staff. A development bank must therefore be prepared to offer attractive terms. One result may be, as was the case in Turkey, that personnel will leave government enterprises to work in the bank. The converse is equally possible. In Chile, enterprises financed or created by the Corporación de Fomento were able to attract staff away from the Corporación, which thus served as a training center for industry.

Personnel requirements will place a heavy administrative overhead on a development bank, a burden which time may not relieve, for the cost of administering investments will increase even though the routines of reviewing applications become simpler. It is possible, and indeed tempting, to overload the staff of a development bank.

But the danger of the reverse is also present. In Ethiopia, considerations of economy led to understaffing the Development Bank. As a result, it plays no important part in seeking out investment opportunities but waits for applications, which in such a country are few and far between (except for routine farm credit). Nor is it in a position to be of much assistance to prospective borrowers through the study of their applications or to assist borrowers after loans have been made.

Profitability of the Bank

The high administrative costs in which a development bank will be involved raise at once the question whether it should try to make a profit. This question has a direct bearing on its criteria for selecting investments, the kind of investments to be made and the charges for loans or other services.

If a development bank is privately owned and is to be effective in mobilizing private capital, it must make or give promise of making a profit. Circumstances in underdeveloped countries are not such as to call forth the voluntary donations of capital, with no expectation of returns, which some New England communities have managed to produce. The necessity of earning a return sufficient to attract the capital the development bank needs and to build up adequate reserves will influence the choice of investments and the level of interest rates and charges. In a privately-owned but government-sponsored development bank, the profit motive may be diluted by more general objectives consistent with governmental policy. In some banks, the shareholders have accepted dividend limitations, though these are sometimes linked to a guaranteed minimum dividend. Even where the development bank has a large component of government capital, it will be necessary to make a profit for the private shareholders, though it may be unnecessary to pay a return on government capital. In some cases the capitalization of development banks is so arranged that neither dividends nor interest are due on the government contribution. But even where a government desires no return, it has a choice of arranging the affairs of the development bank so that it will simply break even (anything less would surely be unacceptable) or so that it will make a profit that can be used to build up reserves and hence the investing capacity of the bank.

It may be argued that the viability of a development bank is much less important that the viability of the enterprises it finances. But if those enterprises are financed in a way that makes economic sense, with due regard to the cost of, or an appropriate return on, capital, the investing institution will itself earn a fair return on its capital investment. It may also be argued that the main issue is how efficiently a development bank is run, not whether it makes a profit. But efficiency of operation requires, at the very least, that the bank be able to cover its costs and set aside a fair amount as reserves. Finally, a government may wish to provide a subsidy to certain economic sectors. There is to start with a significant component of subsidy in the capital provided by development banks. It is being provided where it may not have been available at all before or only on very onerous terms. It is being provided despite substantial, sometimes unmeasurable, risks. Long-term funds are always risky; when made available to small firms, they are riskier still; and they are most risky of all when invested in a new enterprise in a new field. Should a development bank go further and provide funds at an interest rate which is obviously lower than the cost of capital?

In some underdeveloped countries entrepreneurs have been disturbed by the fact that the interest rate on loans from development banks has not been as low as they would like it to be. Governments, in setting up development banks, often think in terms of providing capital very cheaply. This was, for instance, the view in Turkey, where a flat low rate of interest was fixed for all loans. But is it wise to go below the six or eight per cent (already a subsidized rate) which is fairly normal for short-term funds in underdeveloped countries and which is also the rate at which many governments must borrow? Even that rate would have to be supplemented by a percentage of profits, on any fair assessment of costs and risks. But a lower rate is likely to be so far from reflecting the real cost of capital in the country concerned that it would excessively distort the financial results of the undertaking and the pattern of investment. Secondly, to the extent that the rate is subsidized, the opportunities for mobilizing private capital through the development bank will be adversely affected and it will have to rely more heavily on government contributions at a moment when there is no shortage of other objects of government expenditure. This, moreover, would run directly contrary to the purpose of those development banks which seek to strengthen the private sector not only by encouraging private capital into industrial investment but also by attracting it into the development bank itself. Thirdly, the additional three to five per cent which would be charged in the absence of an outright financial subsidy is not likely to exercise a discouraging influence on industrial investment, except in the case of marginal investors. A low interest rate is of even less significance in the inflationary conditions that are more common than not in developing countries. In fact, as already noted, some entrepreneurs appear to prefer to borrow from moneylenders at a much higher rate than is charged by development banks, to avoid the questions and inspections normally required by the latter. Thus a subsidized interest rate for industry has serious disadvantages and little to recommend it.

The question of a subsidized lending rate has wider implications when the development bank is but one of several institutions providing long-term finance, for a bank prepared to offer capital far below cost will be able to compete on unequal terms with others. Generally, development banks are set up to supplement, not to replace, existing banking institutions. One that cuts deeply into the legitimate business of conventional banks may find a main source of finance dried up and may only weaken institutions which in fact need strengthening. The Industrial Finance Corporation of Pakistan is expressly forbidden to lend for a project which can be financed through normal banking channels. The policy of the Japan Development Bank is "to hold down lending to the necessary minimum by making such supplemental loans only as are beyond the capacity of ordinary financial institutions and truly unavailable"; and even in such cases it tries to form syndicates to bring other banks into the operation.

There are thus several good reasons for insisting that a development bank, government-owned or not, should be a profit-making venture (which, incidentally, is not the same as a venture which seeks to make a killing in its investments). In the first place, if the institution takes the kind of risks it ought to take, it is bound to sustain losses on some of its investments. It needs profits from others to build up reserves from which to cover these losses; and since it cannot tell in advance which investments will be losers, it must seek a profit from every one. Secondly, if they are not all distributed as dividends, profits will permit the development bank to increase its investment resources. Thirdly, if a development bank is interested in selling from its portfolio, it must try to set up each investment on a potentially saleable basis. A saleable basis implies that the expected income from the investment will be attractive to the market. Fourthly, a development bank at some time or another—perhaps frequently, if it is successful—is likely to have to borrow from the market. It can do so only if it has a record of profitable investments. It could of course borrow, as many development banks do, with the guarantee of the government behind it; but in view of the many demands on it, a government will not wish to engage its credit if it does not have to. To the extent that a development bank can stand on its own feet, the government's credit can be used for other purposes. Fifthly, a government-owned development bank in particular is likely to come under public and parliamentary fire to the extent that it runs losses. Its continued independence might well depend on a showing of efficient operation without continuing losses of capital. Finally, if the object of a development bank is to stimulate the private sector, it will try to stimulate the financial community as well. By providing capital on conditions commensurate with its cost and with the risks incurred, it can show by example that long-term investment can be both sound and profitable.

Many of the issues raised here concerning the ownership, structure and purposes of a new investment institution are presumably disposed of in its charter. But the charter rarely reflects actual operations; and the most difficult problems—operational policies, criteria for investment, selection of personnel, quality of management—call for action after the statutes are written. An understanding of why investment institutions fail or succeed requires an examination not simply of statutes and balance sheets but mainly of the ways in which the institutions work, the methods by which they reach decisions, the economic environment in which they operate and the concrete problems they face. After five years of dealing with such problems, the Indonesian State Bank for Industry felt impelled "to warn over-ambitious people not to take these difficulties lightly." Fortunately there are by this time many development banks in advanced and in underdeveloped countries alike, in operation for many years, to whose experience appeal can be made by those who face the problems of creating and running such institutions.

An appeal to experience will show that a development bank can do much to strengthen the private sector of an economy, as a means of rapid development. The private sector, however, has many needs and many deficiencies, of which capital is not always or everywhere the most important. To serve these needs and compensate for the deficiencies, many instruments—financial, legal, institutional, etc.,—are needed. No one institution can provide them all. Development banks, hand-tailored to fit the circumstances that bring them forth, are among the institutions that may relieve some of the deficiencies of the private sector. Perhaps the most important are, not finance, but enterprise and managerial and technical skills. In underdeveloped countries the business community and the bankers in particular can rarely be taught any new tricks of trade or finance. What they lack and what a development bank can help to provide are the attitudes and skills required to direct private savings into productive enterprises no less profitable in the long run than the traditional uses of savings and much more important to rapid development.

Tailoring to the requirements of the country and flexibility to meet the needs of the enterprises to be financed are but the first requisites of a development bank. Beyond these, the institution must have skilled and experienced management with an opportunity to exercise independent judgment imaginatively, management which can combine the requirements of an "institutional conscience" with the venturesomeness essential to a vigorous private sector. In such a framework and under such direction, a development bank can have a substantial and beneficial influence on the private sector and on economic development.

Appendices

Selected List
of Development Banks

A LIST OF DEVELOPMENT BANKS could be useful to those concerned with setting up and managing such banks. So many banks exist already and have existed for so long a time that a wealth of experience may be drawn upon for guidance. The experience of no single development bank is likely to provide all the solutions to the problems of another half way around the world or even across the border. It is equally likely, however, that comparable problems have arisen elsewhere and have been dealt with in a suggestive way. Certainly there is no basis for the comment of the management of the State Bank for Industry of Indonesia that, in organizing that bank, there were no precedents to appeal to.[1]

Unfortunately, such a list raises two problems. What institutions should be included? And what can be found out about them? The first arises from the difficulty of definition, the second from the lack of case studies of development banks.

As for definition, the list that follows includes only institutions (public and private) whose purpose is to provide capital and enterprise to private industry. As for information, the list includes some institutions about which much has been written (such as the ICFC of the United Kingdom) and others about which very little is to be found in print, aside from their statutes and annual reports. Moreover, development banks have been selected without reference to their quality or to the importance of their contribution to develop-

[1] *Bank Industri Negara 1951-1956*, p. 86

ment, for lessons, perhaps the more important ones, may be learned from failures as well as successes.

The list is necessarily incomplete and can serve only as a suggestion for those who wish to explore the experience of institutions devoted to the fostering of private enterprise. It is most incomplete in respect of the institutions of advanced countries; it does not include the many private institutions of the capital market, but only some of those sponsored or blessed by government, which may be of special interest because they appear to have relevance for the present problems of underdeveloped countries.

A. Institutions with Which the World Bank Has Been Associated

In the past eight years the World Bank has provided technical advice in the creation of the several development banks cited below. For three of these the Bank has granted loans which take the form of lines of credit. The Bank has assisted and made loans to other development banks, but only as a means of providing finance for pre-agreed projects; these latter are not listed here.

Development Bank of Ethiopia
Development Finance Corporation of Ceylon
Industrial Credit and Investment Corporation of India
Industrial Development Bank of Turkey
Instituto de Fomento Económico of Panama
Instituto de Fomento Nacional of Nicaragua

B. Institutions in Advanced Countries, for Domestic Finance

A.B. Industriekredit, Sweden
Crédit National, France
Den Norske Industribank, Norway
Development Credit Corporations of the New England States, United States
Finance Corporation for Industry, United Kingdom
Iceland Bank of Development, Iceland
Industrial and Commercial Finance Corporation, United Kingdom
Industrial Development Bank of Canada
Industrial Finance Department of the Commonwealth Bank of Australia
Industriekreditbank, A.G., Germany
Istituto per la Ricostruzione Industriale, Italy

Istituto per lo Sviluppo Economico dell'Italia Meridionale, Italy

Istituto Mobiliare Italiano, Italy

Istituto Regionale per Finanziamenti Industriali Siciliani, Italy

Kreditanstalt für Wiederaufbau, Germany

Maatschappij tot Financiering van het Nationaal Herstel N.V.

(Herstelbank), Netherlands

Mediobanca, Italy

Organization for Financing Economic Development, Greece

Reconstruction Finance Corporation, United States

Small Business Administration, United States

Société Nationale de Crédit à l'Industrie, Belgium

C. Institutions in Advanced Countries, for Finance in Underdeveloped Countries

Caisse Centrale de la France d'Outre-Mer, France

Colonial Development Corporation, United Kingdom

Commonwealth Development Finance Company, United Kingdom

D. Institutions in Underdeveloped Countries

1. AFRICA

BELGIAN CONGO
Société de Crédit au Colonat et à l'Industrie

ETHIOPIA
Development Bank

GOLD COAST
Industrial Development Corporation

NIGERIA
Federal Loans Board

Regional Development Boards and Corporations

NORTHERN RHODESIA
Industrial Loans Board

UGANDA
Uganda Development Corporation

UNION OF SOUTH AFRICA
Industrial Development Corporation of South Africa

2. ASIA

BURMA
Industrial Development Corporation
Mineral Resources Development Corporation

CEYLON
Agricultural and Industrial Credit Corporation
Development Finance Corporation
State Mortgage Bank

INDIA
  Industrial Credit and Investment Corporation
  Industrial Finance Corporation
  National Industrial Development Corporation
  State Finance Corporations
INDONESIA
  Bank Industri Negara
JAPAN
  Japan Development Bank
  Long-Term Credit Bank
  People's Finance Corporation
  Industrial Bank

PAKISTAN
  Industrial Development Corporation
  Industrial Finance Corporation
PHILIPPINES
  National Development Company
  Rehabilitation Finance Corporation
THAILAND
  National Economic Development Corporation
  Industrial Bank

3. LATIN AMERICA

ARGENTINA
  Banco Industrial de la República
BOLIVIA
  Corporación Boliviana de Fomento
BRAZIL
  Banco Nacional de Desenvolvimento Econômico
  Banco do Nordeste do Brasil
  Agricultural and Industrial Credit Department of the Banco do Brasil
BRITISH GUIANA
  Credit Corporation
CHILE
  Corporación de Fomento de la Producción
  Instituto de Crédito Industrial
  Caja de Crédito Minero
COLOMBIA
  Corporación Nacional de Producción

  Caja de Crédito Agrario, Industrial y Minero
CUBA
  Banco de Fomento Agrícola e Industrial
ECUADOR
  Banco Nacional de Fomento
  Comisión de Valores
EL SALVADOR
  Instituto Salvadoreño de Fomento de la Producción
GUATEMALA
  Instituto de Fomento de la Producción
HAITI
  Institut Haïtien de Crédit Agricole et Industriel
HONDURAS
  Banco Nacional de Fomento
JAMAICA
  Industrial Development Corporation

MEXICO
Nacional Financiera
NICARAGUA
Instituto de Fomento Nacional
PANAMA
Instituto de Fomento Económico
PERU
Banco de Fomento Agropecuario
Banco Industrial
Banco Minero

PUERTO RICO
Industrial Development Company
Government Development Bank
SURINAM
Finance Corporation for National Reconstruction
VENEZUELA
Corporación Venezolana de Fomento
Industrial Bank

4. MIDDLE EAST

EGYPT
Industrial Bank
IRAQ
Industrial Bank
ISRAEL
Anglo-Palestine Bank

JORDAN
Development Bank
LEBANON
Industrial, Agricultural and Real Estate Credit Bank
TURKEY
Industrial Development Bank

Summary Descriptions
of Some Development Banks

FIVE DEVELOPMENT BANKS are described in order to illustrate various ways in which development banks are set up and financed and in which they operate. The institutions chosen include those most frequently referred to in the preceding text. Each differs from the others, sometimes less in original purpose than in how that purpose is reflected in statutory provisions and (most of all) in actual operation. What follows are the bare facts of the institutions, without an effort to evaluate them.

A. The Industrial Development Bank of Turkey

The Industrial Development Bank (IDB) of Turkey was established after a year of concerted effort and discussion by Turkish private interests, the Turkish Government and the World Bank. It appeared that the growth of private industry was handicapped by the absence of medium- and long-term credit facilities and that it was desirable to create a new institution to provide them. The upshot was the establishment of the IDB in June 1950 and the negotiation of a loan from the World Bank in October of that year.

Purposes of the IDB

The statutes of the IDB set forth its purposes in the following terms:

> A. To support and stimulate the establishment of new private enterprises and the expansion and modernization of existing private enterprises in Turkey.

B. To encourage and assist the participation of private capital, both domestic and foreign, in industry established in Turkey.

C. To encourage and promote the private ownership of securities pertaining to Turkish industry and to assist in the development of a securities market in Turkey.

The IDB is specifically authorized to make loans of any duration with or without security; to participate in private industrial enterprises; in exceptional cases, to establish new enterprises on its own account; to provide technical and administrative assistance to its clients; to sell out its participations "as rapidly as practicable in order to make re-available the resources of the Bank." The IDB is to promote the capital market by creating a market for its own shares and bonds and by stimulating the sale of the securities of the institutions it finances.

Financial Resources of the IDB

The share capital of the IDB was set at T.L. 12.5 million (equivalent to about $4.5 million at the official rate of exchange). This sum was determined not by the requirements of the institution but by the availability of subscriptions to an institution, unique in Turkey, which was to have an artificially low lending rate and which, by statute, would limit its dividends to 12 per cent. Even to obtain this sum, it was necessary to enact a special law under which the Ministry of Finance guaranteed a minimum annual dividend of six per cent for five years; and in addition the Government and the Central Bank had to bring pressure to bear on commercial banks which took up the bulk of the shares. The initial subscribers were 13 commercial banks, two industrial firms and three trade associations. To supplement the share capital, the Central Bank of Turkey undertook to lend the IDB an additional T.L. 12.5 million and the World Bank made it a loan equivalent to T.L. 25.2 million, so that the IDB had available a total of T.L. 50.2 million (about $17.9 million). The ratio of debt to equity was thus three to one, a ratio to which the IDB was held under the terms of its loan contract with the World Bank.

Shortly after the establishment of the IDB, the Turkish Government and the United States Economic Corporation Administration (ECA) set aside T.L. 54.5 million out of Marshall Plan counterpart funds to make productive loans to private industries. In August 1951, ECA (now ICA) entered into an agreement with the IDB under which the latter agreed to administer this Fund for 15 years. The agreement provided that the IDB would lend from the Fund on the basis of an agreed list of industrial priorities, seeking the most beneficial industrial development of the economy; only after a project satisfied the priority criteria would the IDB apply its own investment banking standards. For this service, the IDB was to retain two and one-half per cent per year out of the six per cent interest on the loans, the remainder reverting to the Fund.[1] This arrangement, unforeseen when the IDB was conceived, more than doubled its lending resources and became a significant factor both in the financing of private industrial development and in the profitability of the IDB. The agency agreement placed no burden of risk on the IDB, while substantially increasing its earning power.

In accordance with IDB's objective of stimulating a capital market, it was understood that the original shareholders were to sell a portion of their holdings to other investors as soon as they could. They were unable to do so for the first several years.

However, at the end of 1953, the share capital of the IDB was doubled to enable it to borrow again from the World Bank. To facilitate subscriptions to this new capital by giving promise of higher earning power, the limitation on debt was relaxed to permit a ratio of four to one instead of the previous three to one. At that time, the IDB (after only one year of operating at a loss) was completing its third year of steadily rising profits, and inflationary conditions in Turkey opened new possibilities for selling equities. In this situation and with the promise that dividends would thereafter be raised to the 12 per cent maximum, the IDB had no difficulty in allotting its new stock issue to more than 200 individuals and institutions. The original shareholders now found the opportunity to dispose of some of their holdings. With continued active trading at high premium prices, the number of shareholders has now in-

---

[1] Until the resources of the Fund were fully invested, the IDB was to receive a flat T.L. 500,000 per year plus one and one-quarter per cent of the loans outstanding. When the Fund was fully invested, the flat commission and proportional fee were replaced by the commission of two and one-half per cent. This was raised to three per cent when the interest rate was increased to seven per cent in 1953.

creased to well over 400 and the holdings of the commercial banks have declined from 77.8 per cent of total capital to about 54 per cent.

Simultaneously the Marshall Plan Private Enterprise Fund was increased by T.L. 20 million and the Finance Ministry assisted the IDB in arranging for another internal loan, thus doubling the amount of bonded indebtedness. The entire internal debt of T.L. 25 million has all been taken up by the Central Bank and the State Pension Fund, both of which were reluctant to do so and yielded only to government pressure. Private bond sales have been impossible in Turkey's inflationary situation and in view of the ceiling on the IDB's lending rate.

Since 1955, ICA has made foreign exchange available to private industrial enterprise through the agency of the IDB. The exchange is sold by the IDB (at a profit) according to strict criteria laid down by ICA. These sales are often linked to loans in domestic currency.

Management and Staff of the DB

The statutes vest full powers over policy and organization in a seven-member Board of Directors elected every three years by the shareholders. As a *quid pro quo* for its undertaking to grant certain loans to the IDB, the Central Bank has the right to participate in the selection of one of the seven members. That one is chosen by the shareholders themselves from a panel picked by the Central Bank "from the shareholders and belonging to the banking profession." The Government itself has no rights with regard to board membership or election, a fact which reflected an informal understanding that the Government would take no part in the policy-making or operations of the IDB. A government voice is heard, however, through the Iş Bank, the largest single shareholder, in which the Government and the Democratic Party exercise great influence.

The first Board (named in the statutes) was hand-picked by a few of the founding shareholders and representatives of the Central Bank, the Treasury and the World Bank. Its members, chosen for experience and competence in banking, industry, trade and law, were unanimously elected. In early 1952, the Government forced the entire Board to resign and a new one (with a single hold-over) was proposed by the Government and elected. In 1955, the Government once again made its influence felt in the selection of a new Board and in the removal of an important member of the staff.

The "general management" of the Bank consists of a General Manager and Assistant General Manager chosen by the Board of Directors. The powers and duties of the General Manager are set in the Board's discretion and the Board has the right to employ him and to dismiss him at will. It may also invite him to attend board meetings. In fact, the General Manager and the Assistant General Manager have been the effective directors of the IDB.

In view of the lack of experience in Turkey in the field of industrial financing, a foreign General Manager was first chosen. He acquired quarters for the IDB, chose an Assistant and staff, and died just as operations were about to begin. Ever since, Turks have acted as General Manager. Only one other official of the IDB was chosen from abroad: a controller-accountant, whose one-year contract was not renewed. For the rest, the management and staff of the IDB have been drawn from Turkish private enterprises, the Civil Service and state enterprises. The higher salaries offered by the IDB were in part at least responsible for the successful recruitment from government service.

The IDB has a staff of about 95 persons, of whom about 40 are executive officers and technicians. They are concentrated in five departments which carry the load of investment analysis and administration: Engineering, Financial Analysis, Economic Research, Participations and Operations. The remainder of the personnel, in the Secretary's, Legal, Accounting and Auditing Departments, are concerned with aspects of administration. In 1952 and 1953, at the invitation of the World Bank, several of the IDB's top staff spent a few months in the United States, partly at the World Bank and partly visiting banks and industrial installations elsewhere.

Procedures of the IDB

To assure coordination of the departments and to advise the management, much of the work of the IDB is done through five committees. The top Credit Committee consists of the heads of the main departments under the chairmanship of the Assistant General Manager. It submits recommendations through the General Manager to the Board of Directors for final action. The Board has final authority in all operations, with but two qualifications. First, investment projects for which the funds of the World Bank would be used require approval of the latter as well, although since 1954 projects calling for no more than $50,000 are exempted from prior approval. The participation of the World Bank has only once led to a difference of opinion, when the two institutions differed on the prospects of the Turkish textile industry. Second, the power of final approval of loans under T.L. 50,000 for automotive repair shops has been delegated to the Credit Committee.

The IDB requires applicants to complete a detailed questionnaire before it studies a project. It considers the technical and economic soundness of the project itself, its financial viability, its contribution "to the economic development of the country," and the character and capabilities of the promoters of the project. To assist in this examination and to determine the fields of investment most likely to benefit the country and the potential investor, the Economic Research Department conducts studies of various sectors of the Turkish economy.

The use of the Marshall Plan Private Enterprise Fund is governed by other criteria and by a specific list of industrial priorities (including mining and shipping) laid down by the Government and ICA. Accordingly, the IDB's own and borrowed resources tend to concentrate in some industries, while counterpart funds go into others. Where the IDB has a choice, it naturally tends to use counterpart funds for riskier projects, for the bank carries no risk in the use of those funds.

The staff of the IDB works with applicants in the preparation of the required data and in determining the most suitable financial structure for the enterprise to be financed. After loans are granted, regular reports are required and representatives of the IDB make at least one technical and financial inspection trip annually to the larger enterprises, until the loans have been repaid. Often such visits uncover problems or difficulties requiring corrective measures, which the IDB tries to persuade the enterprise to adopt. On occasion, the enterprise is forced to do so, if the provisions of the loan agreement permit. Its freedom of action in this respect is limited, however, not only by its loan agreements but also by the prevailing financial practices of the country.

Operations of the IDB

LOANS. From the beginning of operations in March 1951 to the end of 1956, the IDB received 1,993 loan applications totalling T.L. 696 million. More than one-third were received in 1951. Thereafter the applications ran at about 250 per year, putting a heavy burden on a modest staff, until 1956, when they fell to 175. A large proportion of these applications is cancelled or rejected, generally because insufficient information has been submitted or because applicants are unwilling to submit to the inspection and information requirements incident to a loan or because they are "impracticable, from economic, technical and financial points of view." Almost half the applications were for small amounts, T.L. 50,000 or less, though they constituted only 2.4 per cent of the total financing sought.

From the 1,993 applications, 340 loans have been granted for a total of T.L. 161.6 million. Somewhat over half of all loans granted (T.L. 83.1 million) have been financed from the Marshall Plan Private Enterprise Fund; and about 28 per cent (T.L. 46 million) from the proceeds of the two World Bank loans. The remainder have been met from the IDB's own resources. Almost one-third of all loans granted have been very small (under T.L. 50,000 each), most of them for automotive repair shops. The largest volume of loans has gone to textiles, food processing, building materials, metal ore smelting and chemicals. Although in the early years loans were given primarily to well-established industries (such as textiles), they are now given almost exclusively to new or less well-developed industries (such as chemicals, foundry products, automotive repair shops, etc.).

The use of the World Bank loan was severely limited during the first two years, because of the problem created by the foreign exchange risk implicit in World Bank loans. [2] This risk the Government would not, and the IDB felt it could not, assume; and borrowers would not accept a dollar risk for European purchases, especially as long as European exchange was fairly readily available through EPU arrangements. The problem was not resolved until early 1953, after

[2] See pp. 66-68 for a discussion of foreign exchange risk.

foreign exchange had again become tight. An agreement was then reached between the IDB and the Central Bank, under which the latter, by forward foreign exchange sales, in effect shouldered the risk. The IDB passed on the cost of this service by charging its borrowers a fixed fee. Thereafter, borrowed foreign exchange was used at a more rapid rate and the IDB was able to increase its lending operations.

The Bank's loans run from three to 12 years, the average term being seven years. The term is calculated by assuming that the borrower, who is expected in fact to earn something like 20 to 25 per cent a year, will take as profit only 10 to 15 per cent. The remainder, together with depreciation allowances, is assumed to be available for debt service; it must be enough to repay the loan in eight to 10 years. All loans are secured, but the amount of the loan can be no more than 50 per cent of the appraised value of the mortgaged property. The borrower is required to have at least 30 to 50 per cent of his capital in equity. A flat interest rate is charged. Until September 1953 it was six per cent; thereafter it was raised to seven per cent. A one per cent commitment fee is also levied. A grace period of up to 18 months is normally allowed.

PARTICIPATIONS. At the end of 1955, the IDB's participations amounted to a mere T.L. 1 million. By the end of 1956, they had risen to T.L. 4.6 million and another T.L. 5.7 million had been approved or were under consideration. Two factors have inhibited this type of financing. At the start, the IDB deliberately avoided participations because it felt such risky operations should wait until it had acquired some experience and had built up some reserves. When, in 1952 and after, the IDB was willing to take participations, it found entrepreneurs generally unwilling to share ownership. Only in the past two years has the attitude towards joint ventures begun to change. The IDB has itself become more anxious to engage in such investments as a means of protecting itself against inflation.

COMMERCIAL LOANS. In 1954, the Bank started to make short-term commercial loans, chiefly for working capital for the enterprises to which it has made medium- and long-term loans. By the end of 1956, the amount outstanding stood at T.L. 27.6 million. The Bank grants such loans in order to use temporarily idle funds; but the expressed intention to expand this line of activity as resources increase suggests that the Bank finds such loans quite lucrative. Normal commercial lending is within the statutory authority of the Bank, but contrary to the original intention to supplement rather than compete with the operations of the regular banks which helped set up the IDB.

Financial Results of Operation

The statutes provide that, from net profits, five per cent must be set aside for "legal reserve funds" and another five per cent as a "reserve for contingent losses." Only thereafter may a six per cent dividend be paid. If some net profits still remain, specified percentages are to be paid out to the founders of the IDB, the Board of Directors and the employees, after which a second six per cent dividend may be declared and the remainder allocated to the "extraordinary reserve fund."

In its first year, the IDB incurred a loss and its shareholders decided to forgo the dividend for which they might have called on the Finance Ministry. In the second year (the first of operations) there was a small profit, and the IDB called on the Government to make up a six per cent dividend. Thereafter profits rose rapidly and the IDB was able to pay its own dividends, while simultaneously repaying the Treasury. In 1954, 1955 and 1956, it paid out the maximum 12 per cent. Meantime, it had built up its reserves to T.L. 4.1 million, three-quarters of it added in 1955 and 1956. The management of the IDB is strongly disposed to building up the bank's reserves. In 1956, net profits totalled T.L. 4.9 million, a return of 26 per cent on paid-in capital.

Economic Results

The IDB has become, over the past several years, the most important single factor in financing private industry in Turkey. Certainly a part of the investment it helped to finance would have occurred in any event, for factors other than the existence of the IDB helped to call it forth. Nevertheless, its contribution has been unmistakable and quantitatively large. On the side of financing, the investments it has helped to finance have accounted in various years for 10 to 25 per cent of all private industrial investment. The IDB's own estimates are that its loans and participations of T.L. 172 million were linked with additional investments by its clients of T.L. 175 million in fixed assets and T.L. 105 million in working capital. The expected output of T.L. 732 million from this investment would add about 30 per cent to the value of industrial production in 1955. The enterprises it financed until 1954 were estimated to yield a private profit averaging 30 per cent and a social return of about 23 per cent.

The IDB has also contributed through assistance to its applicants and clients in the preparation of projects and the improvement of accounting procedures and technical and management practices. Its contribution to the growth of the capital market was delayed but is increasingly apparent. Whatever discount caution impels one to apply to these facts in consideration of other contributing factors, the significance of the IDB to the Turkish economy and to the private industrial sector in particular remains very great.

B.   Three Development Banks in India

THE CENTRAL GOVERNMENT OF INDIA has sponsored the establishment of a battery of development banks to help to finance and stimulate the private industrial sector of the Indian economy. The question of financial aids to industry, by no means new to India, received a new fillip after Partition. Shortly thereafter, in July 1948, the Industrial Finance Corporation (IFC) was established to make medium- and long-term investments in circumstances where recourse to normal banking channels or to the capital market was inappropriate or impracticable. The vast area of the country, the overwhelming prevalence of small enterprises and the difficulty an institution faces in dealing with both large and small firms led to the enactment in 1951 of a law providing for the establishment of development banks in the States designed to finance small enterprises. Since then, 13 State Finance Corporations have come into existence. Apparently convinced that the mere provision of finance was not enough to vitalize the industries whose expansion or creation was called for in the Five-Year Plan, particularly in new and relatively untried fields, the Central Government established the National Industrial Development Corporation (NIDC) in October 1954. This institution, with wide powers to finance, promote and manage both public and private enterprises, was intended to act as a "pathfinder," to lead the way in developing the new industries which "harmonious development" required. A few months later, in January 1955, the Industrial Credit and Investment Corporation (ICICI) was established to stimulate private industry and to increase the flow of foreign private capital to India. The ICICI is intended to supplement the other two nation-wide institutions by stressing equity investment, especially by development of underwriting machinery in cooperation with other institutions of the capital market, and by encouraging foreign investment.

Aside from the finance provided by these special institutions, capital has also been made available to industries by direct grants, loans and equity participations by the Government. Moreover, the older and more conventional financial institutions of India are active, directly and indirectly, in contributing to medium-term industrial finance.

Of the three special nation-wide development banks, the IFC (although in effect controlled by the Government) is jointly owned by the Government, the Reserve Bank and private institutions; the NIDC, by the Government alone; and the ICICI by private interests, foreign and domestic.

1. THE INDUSTRIAL FINANCE CORPORATION

Purposes of the IFC

The preamble of the IFC Act sets forth its purpose as "making medium- and long-term credits more readily available to industrial concerns in India, particularly in circumstances where normal banking accommodation is inappropriate or recourse to capital-issue methods is impracticable." To this end, it is authorized (under the original Act and its subsequent amendments) to guarantee for periods not exceeding 25 years loans floated in the market by industrial concerns; to underwrite the issue of stock, shares, bonds and debentures of industrial concerns; to retain whatever securities may be necessary as an incident of underwriting but (unless it has government permission) for not more than seven years; and to grant loans or advances to, or subscribe to debentures of, industrial concerns, repayable within 25 years. The IFC may not subscribe to stock or buy the equity of any company or participate in its management.

State enterprises are excluded from the operations of the IFC and its power to finance private industry is restricted to limited companies and cooperative societies engaged in manufacturing, mining, production and distribution of electric power and shipping.

Financial Resources of the IFC

The authorized capital was set at Rs. 100 million (equivalent to about $21 million at the official rate), of which half was immediately issued and the remainder was to be issued with the approval of the Government whenever the IFC saw fit. Shares were to be held as follows: the Government and the Reserve Bank, 20 per cent each; scheduled banks, 25 per cent; insurance companies and other financial institutions, 25 per cent; and the remaining 10 per cent, cooperative banks. While actual holdings have fluctuated somewhat, their distribution has always approximated the allotments set forth in the Act. (However, the nationalization of certain financial institutions has given the Government a larger voice than was originally intended.) No individual holds, or is permitted to hold, shares. The Government guaranteed an annual two and one-quarter per cent tax-free dividend on paid-in capital, as well as repayment of principal.

The IFC is authorized to add to its resources by issuing bonds and debentures, up to five times the total of paid-in capital and reserves. The bonds are guaranteed by the Central Government, which also fixes the interest rate on the recommendation of the Board of the IFC. The IFC is also authorized to borrow from abroad, to take deposits of not less than five years up to Rs. 100 million on certain conditions, and to borrow from the Reserve Bank on short term. The Government undertook to make up any loss deriving from foreign exchange fluctuations.

As of the middle of 1956, the IFC had borrowed Rs. 78 million (at three and one-quarter per cent) from the public against government-guaranteed bonds and debentures and had Rs. 8.2 million outstanding from the Reserve Bank. It had not borrowed from abroad, and it had not accepted deposits. Since mid-1956, the IFC has borrowed substantial sums from the Government, in addition to the amount required to pay its guaranteed dividend, in order to increase its investment resources.

Management and Staff of the IFC

The direction of the IFC is vested in a Board of Directors aided by a Central Committee and a General Manager. The Board is instructed to "act on business principles due regard being had by it to the interest of industry, commerce and the general public." Provision was also made for the Board to be "guided by such instructions on questions of policy as may be given to it by the Central Government." If the instructions are not carried out, the Government may supersede the Board and appoint a new one. The Government is thus in a position to define and enforce the policy of the IFC and is authorized to make rules to give effect to the provisions of the Act.

The Board consists of 13 members, of whom four are named by the Central Government and two by the Reserve Bank. Six others are elected, two by the scheduled banks, two by the cooperative banks and two by the insurance companies and other financial institutions. The remaining director is the Chairman of the Board, a "stipendiary" official named by the Government; he is the executive officer of the IFC. The Central Committee, which acts for the Board, consists of five members of the Board under the chairmanship of the Chairman of the Board. The General Manager is appointed by the Government on recommendation of the Board. The Government may remove him at any time but the Board may remove him only under certain conditions.

The present organization and division of authority reflect the last of a series of changes brought about in large part by parliamentary criticism of the operations of the IFC and of the power of the former Managing Director vis-à-vis the Board of Directors.

Operations of the IFC

Until July 1956, the IFC had not undertaken any guarantees or underwriting operations. Loans authorized amounted at that time to Rs. 432 million, representing 208 loans to 154 companies. More than half the loans were for new enterprises rather than for the expansion of old. Of the total, however, only Rs. 167 million had been disbursed. Almost one-third of the remainder had been withdrawn by the IFC or declined by the borrowers. The sugar industry has been the main beneficiary of IFC loans, with more than one-quarter of the total. For the rest, the loans are distributed among a large number of industries, chiefly textiles, industrial chemicals, paper and cement. The largest number of loans has been granted to enterprises in Bombay State, but recently the IFC has apparently sought to increase lending in areas which have not yet received much aid. A substantial number of small loans has been made, some for working capital as well as for the acquisition of fixed assets. Almost half of all loans are of less than Rs. 100,000 each, but they account for only one-eighth of the value of loans authorized. One-third of the borrowers were in this smallest category. Twenty-five per cent of all loans were in the category of Rs. 400,000 to Rs. 500,000. In order to prevent overlapping between the operations of the IFC and those of the State Finance Corporations, agreement has recently been reached on a lower limit for IFC investments. The IFC's loans in any State will be a minimum of Rs. 1 million each or an amount greater than the statutory maximum of the State Finance Corporation's lending power, whichever is less. No single loan may, under the law, exceed Rs. 10 million unless it has a specific government guarantee.

Of the total number of enterprises financed, six have defaulted on principal (one has since been sold and one leased) and about 6.4 per cent of the amount of interest due is in default.

Until February 1952, the IFC charged on its loans interest of five and one-half per cent, of which one-half per cent was returned to the borrower if interest and principal payments were made when due. Since then the interest rate has been raised to six and one-half per cent, with the same conditional rebate. A commitment charge is also made.

The Central Committee approves all loans. Applications are examined from a technical, financial and managerial viewpoint, all in close cooperation with government departments in order to assure conformity with government policy. All loans (and guarantees) must be fully secured by a first mortgage. A loan may not exceed 40 to 50 per cent of the value of the fixed assets mortgaged. Expenditure is closely controlled and inspections are made. The IFC usually appoints a director to the board of the borrowing concern.

The IFC follows the policy directives and regulations issued to it from time to time by the Government. The directives include requirements of government approval for sale of a defaulted property and of publication in the Annual Report of all data regarding loans and borrowers. Another directive requires that "a minimum margin of 50 per cent should be generally aimed at and greater attention should be given to the proper assessment of the earning capacity of the borrowing concern."

Financial Results

The IFC is required to establish a reserve fund and may pay a dividend if it has a net profit. However, until the reserve fund equals the paid-in capital and until government advances have been repaid, the dividend may not exceed two and one-quarter per cent. Thereafter it may not exceed five per cent. If there is an excess of profits, they must go to the Central Government. Dividends due the Government and the Reserve Bank go into a Special Reserve Fund, until the total of the two reserve funds reaches Rs. 5 million.

In every year thus far, the Government has been called upon to make up the guaranteed two and one-quarter per cent dividend. The debt accruing to the Government for such dividends now totals Rs. 5.3 million. Meantime, modest reserves have been set aside; on June 30, 1956, they amounted to Rs. 6.2 million.

2. THE NATIONAL INDUSTRIAL DEVELOPMENT CORPORATION

THE NIDC HAS HARDLY BEGUN OPERATIONS thus far and little can be said about it other than to describe what it is meant to do. Indeed, as of this moment, it is not easy to say whether the institution will turn out to be a "development bank" in the sense in which that term has here been used. There is an ambivalence in discussions of its role which, without diminishing its potential importance to the economy, leaves some doubt whether it will develop as an agent for government planning and investment or as an aid to the private sector.

The main objective of the NIDC is development rather than finance. It is intended primarily to plan and stimulate the creation of enterprises which are considered basic to industrialization and the absence of which constitutes an obstacle to development. The provision of capital is considered secondary to the NIDC's role as planner and promoter. Working closely in accordance with the Five-Year Plan, the NIDC is intended to take the lead in filling gaps in India's industrial structure and to provide finance only to industries created for that purpose. It is authorized to promote, establish and operate enterprises; to advance industrial development; to aid, assist and finance industrial undertakings, whether owned or managed by the Government or by private firms; and to take up the study and investigation of industrial schemes and to seek to implement them.

To attain these objectives, the NIDC is authorized:

    i. to render assistance in the shape of capital, credit, machinery, equipment or any other type of facility,

    ii. to grant loans and advances to industries, subscribe to, underwrite or deal in shares and debentures of companies, and also to guarantee loans and advances to industries, as well as issues of shares and debentures made by companies,

    iii. to manage, control or supervise a concern by nominating directors or advisers or otherwise collaborating with it, to enter into partnership or any other arrangement for joint working with a concern,

    iv. to act as a Government agency for implementing the policy of granting public loans on some concessional terms to certain industries,

    v. to build up "know-how" in the country by raising a corps of technical, engineering and managerial staff for technical assistance, and

    vi. to bring together project reports on new basic industries and then to assist both private and public sector about the manner in which these industries are to be started and run.

The NIDC must obviously work in close coordination with government plans. The coordination will be facilitated both by the nature of its governing board and by the way in which it will obtain its financial resources. The NIDC's charter provides for a Board of

Directors consisting of 15 to 25 persons, all appointed by the Government. Its chairman is the Minister of Commerce and Industry, and it includes representatives of private concerns. The head of the NIDC is also a member of the Board of the IFC and the Government Director of the ICICI.

The authorized share capital was set at Rs. 10 million (equivalent to about $2.1 million at the official rate). One million rupees have actually been issued and subscribed, all by the Government. This capital can be increased by special resolution. However, the NIDC can receive grants, loans or advances from the Government from which it will in fact derive the bulk of its resources. It can also issue bonds and debentures and accept deposits.

The Second Five-Year Plan calls for the provision of Rs. 550 million from the allotment of the Ministry of Commerce and Industry to the NIDC. About 40 per cent of this sum has already been earmarked for the modernization of the jute and cotton textile industries. The rest is to be used for pioneering new basic and heavy industries. The industries to which the NIDC is to devote itself—in some of which investigations have already begun—include foundry and forge shops, structural fabrication, refractories, chemicals and drugs, aluminum, heavy machinery and rolling mill equipment. Various projects for heavy industries in the public sector have been assigned to the NIDC for study and execution; and others are likely to follow. Foreign firms and experts have been brought into consultation on specific projects; industry-wide committees have been set up in connection with the two textile programs; three loans have already been made to jute plants and others are under consideration.

The impressiveness of the plans lying on the NIDC's door-step is somewhat lessened by the problems it faces in proceeding to carry them out: how to obtain technical personnel, not only to do its own work, but to offer technical advice to all of Indian industry; and how the enterprises it sets up are to be organized and administered.

3. THE INDUSTRIAL CREDIT AND INVESTMENT CORPORATION OF INDIA

Purposes of the ICICI

The Memorandum of Association of the ICICI sets out 46 "objects" for which the ICICI was established, which together give it very broad financial and entrepreneurial powers. The first of these objects sums up the entire list:

> To carry on the business of assisting industrial enterprises within the private sector of industry in India, in general by
>
>   i. assisting in the creation, expansion and modernization of such enterprises,
> ii. encouraging and promoting the participation of private capital, both internal and external, in such enterprises,
> iii. encouraging and promoting private ownership of industrial investments and the expansion of investment markets,
>
> and in particular by
>
>   i. providing finance in the form of long- and medium-term loans or equity participation,
>   ii. sponsoring and underwriting new issues of shares and securities,
> iii. guaranteeing loans from other private investment sources,
>   iv. making funds available for re-investment by revolving investments as rapidly as prudent, and
>   v. furnishing managerial, technical and administrative advice and assisting in obtaining managerial, technical and administrative services to Indian industry.

Financial Resources of the ICICI

The authorized capital of the ICICI is set at Rs. 250 million (equivalent to about $52.5 million at the official rate of exchange), divided into Rs. 50 million of ordinary shares and Rs. 200 million of unclassified shares. The ordinary shares are fully issued, subscribed and paid in. Seventy per cent of the shares were privately placed among Indian, British and American institutions and 30 per cent were issued for public subscription in India in February 1955. The enthusiasm of the response may be judged from the fact that there were 1,100 applications, of which more than half were for less than 20 shares. The ICICI now has more than 2,000 shareholders. (As a result of the nationalization of Indian life assurance companies, the 16 per cent of the stock held by them has passed into the hands of the Government, which, contrary to the original intention, has thus become the largest shareholder. The Government has stated that it will not take advantage of this "adventitious position.")

As may be seen from the following table, the shares were distributed, in accordance with an agreement with the Government, in such manner as to prevent any shareholder or class of shareholders from exercising effective control of the ICICI.

DISTRIBUTION OF SHARES OF THE ICICI

	Rs. Million	%
British institutions................	10	
American institutions.............	5	
Total foreign interests.........		15	30
British and Commonwealth life assurance companies in India.........	1.3	
Indian life assurance companies.....	6.7	
Total life assurance companies in India..................		8	16
Indian investing public............		15	30
Indian banks, directors of ICICI, etc.		12	24
GRAND TOTAL..........		50	100

The British subscription is divided among eight Eastern Exchange Banks, 30 leading insurance companies, the Commonwealth Development Finance Company, Ltd., and five industrial corporations. The American investors are the Bank of America, Rockefeller Bros., the Olin Mathieson Chemical Corporation and Westinghouse International Corporation.

The ICICI's resources have been increased by an advance from the Government and a loan from the World Bank. The charter of the

ICICI authorizes it to borrow up to three times the sum of its un-impaired paid-in capital, its surplus and reserves, and its advance from the Government. Under an agreement consummated in January 1955, the Government advanced Rs. 75 million (the counterpart of a United States Government gift of steel) interest-free for 30 years. This advance must be repaid in 15 equal annual instalments, begin-ning in the sixteenth year. In March 1955, the World Bank made the ICICI a loan equivalent to Rs. 47.6 million, bringing total resources at present to almost Rs. 173 million (about $36.2 million).

Under the terms of the ICICI's agreements with the Government and the World Bank, if the capital of the ICICI, including the government advance, is impaired by 20 per cent, the Government, the ICICI and the Bank are to examine the situation and discuss remedial action; if by 30 per cent, the Government, acting in consulta-tion with the Bank and the ICICI, may apply for a court order to wind up the business of the ICICI. By agreement the obligation to the World Bank ranks first in the event of liquidation; the obligation to the shareholders, second; and the obligation to the Government, last.

Management and Staff of the ICICI

Full power to conduct the business of the ICICI is vested in a Board of Directors of five to 10 persons, elected by the shareholders. The first Board, named in the Articles of Association, was replaced by an elected Board at the first general meeting of shareholders and thereafter one-third of the membership is to be retired and replaced each year. The President of India has the right to name a director as long as any part of the government advance is outstanding; and the holders of any debentures of the ICICI may also name a director to represent them.

The present Board of Directors is made up of nationals of three countries, one from the United States, two from the United Kingdom and the rest from India.

The Board has the authority to appoint (and remove) the manager and staff. The first manager resigned as Chief Cashier of the Bank of England to accept his post; the only other foreigner on the staff is the Technical Director. All others are Indian.

Policies and Procedures of the ICICI

At its first meeting, the Board of Directors adopted the following operational policies:

(a) It will be the policy of the Company not to seek in any enterprise financed by it, a controlling interest or any other interest which would give it primary responsibility for the management of such enterprise. The Company will to the maximum extent possible, consistent with the protection of its interests, and after satisfying itself that qualified and experienced management is and will continue to be available, leave the management in the hands of the enterprise so financed.

(b) With the exception of intermediate investment of its liquid funds in short-term securities, the Company will keep its financing, whether through loans or equity participations or guarantees, diversified, both as among types of undertakings and within any one area of India and normally will not commit more than 10% of its original paid-up share capital and government investment to any single undertaking.

(c) The Company normally will revolve its funds by selling its investments at its discretion whenever it can receive a fair price therefor. In selling such investments the Company will pay due regard both to its own interests and to those of other participants in the particular investment.

(d) In undertaking obligations payable in foreign exchange the Company's management, to the fullest extent possible, will endeavor to cover the foreign exchange risk involved by taking obligations payable in the applicable foreign exchange or by forward exchange or by forward exchange contract or other means.

(e) It will be the policy of the Company to build reserves consistent with sound financial practices.

The principles stated in this declaration were decided upon by the foreign investors, the main Indian investors, the World Bank and the Government, before the ICICI came into existence.

All proposals submitted to the ICICI are carefully examined from the technical and financial points of view. Many requests for assistance have been turned down because the ICICI has decided that it would be not practicable to finance small enterprises or businesses run by partnerships and individuals; and it has found that it cannot assist enterprises in amounts of less than Rs. 500,000. If the amount required by an enterprise is considered too large to be handled by the ICICI, it undertakes to interest other parties in the investment.

The ICICI has devoted considerable attention to the problems of underwriting public capital issues. In this connection it has decided that, as a condition for underwriting, issues must be offered to the general public rather than to a closed circle of promoters and directors. The ICICI is also working on the establishment, in association with other institutions, of a regular organization for underwriting. These efforts to stimulate more orderly procedures of underwriting, to spread its risk and to encourage flotation of issues are likely to be a major part of the ICICI's activities.

Operations of the ICICI

In its first 10 months of operation in 1955, the ICICI agreed to provide financial assistance to 11 applicants and 25 other proposals were under study. Of the 11 applications approved, five related to the underwriting of public issues of ordinary or preferred stock; four called for direct subscriptions to ordinary or preferred stock; and two involved loans. A year later, at the end of 1956, approved investments totalled 25 and amounted to Rs. 60 million. Of this, 10 were loans totalling Rs. 29.5 million; seven were underwritings of ordinary and preferred shares totalling Rs. 23.8 million; and eight were direct subscriptions to ordinary and preferred shares amounting to Rs. 6.8 million. Outstanding disbursed investments as of that date amounted to Rs. 11.5 million in shares and Rs. 5.4 million in loans (all secured by mortgages). The industries in which investments had been made included sugar, paper, chemicals, metal ores, electrical equipment and textiles. At the end of 1956, another 15 applications were under consideration, involving a total of Rs. 60 million. If approved, these would almost exhaust ICICI's rupee resources.

The interest rate on loans has been around six per cent and the charge for underwriting, two per cent plus one per cent brokerage. It has been said that the interest-free government grant permits the ICICI to lend at a rate one per cent lower than would otherwise be the case.

No use has yet been made of the foreign exchange available from the World Bank loan, due to the still unsettled problem of who is to assume the foreign exchange risk. If a borrower required foreign exchange, he was formerly able to purchase it from the Reserve Bank with borrowed rupees and the ICICI had sufficient resources in domestic currency at its disposal. However, in January 1957 the Government found it necessary, in view of the serious tightening in India's foreign exchange position, to impose stringent restrictions on all foreign exchange expenditures. It suggested that attempts be made to obtain foreign exchange credits abroad or from lending institutions in India. Consequently, the ICICI began to accept applications in foreign exchange, and in view of the shortage of exchange it is likely that borrowers will be willing to assume the exchange risk in order to get imported equipment.

Financial Results

The ICICI closed its first year with a substantial profit of Rs. 2.9 million before tax. In 1956, profits before tax amounted to Rs. 3.7 million. These profits, while investment operations were still small, were made possible by the temporary investment both of the advance from the Government and of its own capital, chiefly in short-term government and government-guaranteed securities. Profits may be expected to increase, particularly when equity investments mature.

The Articles of the ICICI provide that, after its fifth year, 25 per cent of profits are to be put into a reserve fund, until the fund is equal to the outstanding amount of the government advance. Although not required to do so, the ICICI set aside for this purpose Rs. 500,000 from the profits of each of its first two years, in accordance with its policy of building up reserves.

There is no guarantee of a dividend to shareholders and none was declared in the first year. However, at the first annual general meeting of stockholders the Chairman of the Board noted that the Directors "recognize the desirability of placing the shares of this company in the dividend list as early as possible, consistent with prudence." At the end of the second year, a three and one-half per cent dividend, free of income tax, was declared.

C. The Nacional Financiera of Mexico

The Nacional Financiera is a complex institution which goes far beyond the ordinary functions of a development bank. No brief statement can do justice to its far-flung operations. It has been one of the main instruments through which the Mexican Government has sought to stimulate and to finance the growth of industry and public utilities, and it has acted as a creator and financier of enterprises, a mobilizer of domestic capital, a channel for foreign lending, a regulator of the stock exchange, and an agent for federal and local governments.

Although the Nacional Financiera was created in 1934, its important role as an instrument of development dates from its reorganization in 1941. In that year, under the pressure of wartime shortages, it began to concentrate on basic industries and sponsored new enterprises in the sugar, iron and steel, pulp, caustic soda, textile and cement industries.

Purposes of the Financiera

The Nacional Financiera was originally set up primarily to help sell government bonds and to assist the newly created market for private securities. As a result of its reorganization in 1941 and of two subsequent modifications of its Organic Law, it is now authorized by its statutes to:

    a. supervise and regulate the national market for securities and long-term loans;

    b. promote the investment of capital in the organization, transformation and merger of all kinds of companies in the country;

    c. operate as an institution providing support for financial or investment enterprises when they extend credit guaranteed by securities;

    d. supervise and direct the operation of stock exchanges;

    e. act as a financial or investment company;

    f. act as a trustee, especially for the Federal Government and its dependencies;

    g. act as agent and counsel for the Federal Government, the States, Municipalities and Official Dependencies in connection with the issuance, negotiation, conversion, etc., of public securities;

h. act as legal depository for all types of securities;
i. act as a savings bank;
j. instruct and advise the National Banking Commission insofar as its work relates to the foregoing or may contribute to its realization;
k. take charge of all negotiation and handling of foreign loans when a guarantee of the Government is required.

In addition, the Financiera is authorized to act as agent of the Government for various other purposes.

The operations of the Financiera thus cover a wide variety of fields, but they are concentrated—so far as economic development is concerned—on the provision of long-term credits to and the purchase of securities in industry and public utilities, the creation of new enterprises in these fields and the channelling of foreign loans.

Financial Resources of the Financiera

The capital of the Nacional Financiera is now (since 1955) 200 million pesos (equivalent to about $16 million at the official rate). The Government permanently holds a small majority and the rest is in the hands of individuals and institutions or available to them with government permission. Financial institutions are required to subscribe to shares up to a specified proportion of their capital and reserves. The Nacional Financiera derives the bulk of its funds, however, from borrowing at home and abroad, often on behalf of various government and semi-government institutions.

As of the end of 1956 the Financiera had obtained from abroad a total of $579 million, of which 82 per cent had been disbursed. More than half came from loans by the Export-Import Bank and most of the rest from the World Bank. So far as the bulk of these foreign resources is concerned, the Financiera simply acted as an intermediary and as a channel for specific projects, often on instructions from the Government. Only a small part of the foreign loans is devoted to the regular operations of the institution.

The two main forms of domestic borrowing have been "participation certificates" and "financing bonds." The participation certificates represent co-ownership of a common fund of securities held by the Financiera as trustee. They bear interest at five per cent (since

1950; before that date the rate was seven and six per cent) and are redeemable at par and on demand. Each issue of participation certificates is backed by designated items in the portfolio of the Nacional Financiera, of which the holders of the certificates are co-owners. The devaluation of 1954 led to a run on the certificates, which in turn forced the Financiera to draw on the Central Bank. In view of this event and of the criticism that the certificates were drawing funds away from deposit and savings accounts, thus diverting the resources of private banks, the Financiera was forced to reexamine the conditions under which certificates were issued. In mid-1956 a new issue was launched, which combined fixed-interest securities with a proportion of equities and had no repurchase clause. The issue was not a great success, although its total yield may be as much as 10 per cent. The securities policy of the Financiera is thus uncertain at this time. At the end of 1956, outstanding certificates amounted to 1.2 billion pesos, a full third of the resources of the Financiera. Half were held by private individuals and companies and the remainder by financial institutions. The financing bonds are direct obligations of the Financiera, denominated in both pesos and dollars, and are tax exempt. They, too, are redeemable at par and are issued at a rate lower than the certificates. Financing bonds outstanding at the end of 1956 amounted to 302 million pesos.

So important and so liquid have both these types of securities been that the banking system uses them, in accordance with Central Bank regulations, as liquid reserves in the way in which Treasury bills are used elsewhere. The effectiveness of the Financiera in borrowing and the strength of its certificates and bonds probably rest on the implicit support of the Government and the Bank of Mexico and the ready recourse which the Financiera has to the latter. The Nacional Financiera has also in the past obtained funds from the Government both for its own operations and for administration on behalf of the Government.

The growth of the Nacional Financiera's resources is illustrated in the following table.

INVESTMENT RESOURCES OF THE NACIONAL FINANCIERA

(in millions of pesos at end of year indicated)

	1941	1945	1950	1955	1956
Internal					
Bonds.............	1.5	16.7	70.4	306.1	302.5
Certificates.........	7.4	222.4	693.6	1,281.6	1,217.8
Other.............	43.9	447.9	408.4	739.7	695.5
Total............	52.8	687.0	1,172.4	2,327.4	2,215.8
External	—	68.6	725.1	1,445.9	1,424.2
GRAND TOTAL.....	52.8	755.6	1,897.5	3,773.3	3,640.0

It is from these resources that the Nacional Financiera makes its investments. In addittition, however, the Nacional Financiera conducts a sizeable agency business both for the Government and for private clients.

Management of the Financiera

The management of the Financiera is vested in a Board of Directors and a General Manager. The Board consists of seven directors and five alternates. Of the regular directors, three are chosen by the Government and four by the private shareholders. The government directors have—each one individually—the right to veto investments involving more than 50,000 pesos and certain other types of operations. These directors are generally public officials (the chairman of the Board is the Finance Minister) and thus provide a means of coordinating the policies of the Government with those of the Financiera.

The Board has full authority to appoint and remove the General Manager and all other staff.

Operations of the Financiera

The main activity of the Nacional Financiera is the financing of industry, by loans and by subscription to securities. In 1941, in line with government policy, the Nacional Financiera started to concentrate on the creation of new industrial enterprises. By the end of the forties, its attention shifted to public utilities, on which it continues to concentrate, if one takes into account the enterprises for which it acts as an intermediary for foreign loans. The outstanding investments (excluding small amounts in agriculture, trade, banks and government) of the Nacional Financiera at the end of 1956 amounted to 3.1 billion pesos, a slight reduction from the level of the two preceding years. Of this total, 1.3 billion pesos were devoted to manufacturing, 0.7 billion pesos to transport, 0.6 billion pesos to power and fuel and 0.3 billion pesos to construction. Seventy-three per cent of these investments took the form of loans, the remainder of securities.

The largest investments of the Financiera are in enterprises in which the Government also participates, but the greatest number are made in purely private undertakings. The largest investments now are in the fields of iron and steel, assembly and production of vehicles, food processing, transport, power and construction. Such enterprises also obtain working capital from the Financiera. The Financiera provides rediscount facilities to Mexico's many private financieras and supports their securities, as well as those of some industries, in the market. Similar support has also been given to various government banks.

In the field of utilities, access to foreign lenders has been of primary importance to the Nacional Financiera. Of the $472 million of foreign loans disbursed by the end of 1956, $283 million have been devoted to transport and communications and $123 million to electric power. The Nacional Financiera also guarantees foreign suppliers' credits and tries to assist domestic enterprises in finding foreign equity.

The initiative in the most important of the Financiera's investments lies in its own staff and in that of the Bank of Mexico. There the large undertakings are formulated. Usually the Financiera then seeks, sometimes successfully, private domestic and foreign participation. The policy of the Financiera is to sell out its undertakings when it can. In fact, relatively few have been sold, for the poor ones find no buyers and the Financiera is reluctant to part with the successful ones.

The Nacional Financiera ordinarily takes no part in the direction of its subsidiaries, other than to appoint a director; but sometimes it also appoints the manager or a technical advisor. In the case of its loans, the institution normally relies on reports and inspections to make sure the loans are being properly used.

Financial Results

The Financiera has produced a profit every year since its creation in 1934. Profits have been divided between reserves and dividends, except in 1947 and 1954 when they were entirely allocated to dividends.

In 1956, profits totalled 108 million pesos, of which 103 million pesos derived from the Investment Department and five million pesos from the Trust Department. Profits for 1956 have not yet been allocated. But of 1955 profits, amounting to 48 million pesos, 73 per cent was allocated to various reserves and a dividend of six per cent was declared on shares held by the Government and a dividend of seven per cent on shares held by the public. The record of profits and dividends is shown below.

PAID-IN CAPITAL, NET PROFITS AND DIVIDENDS OF THE NACIONAL FINANCIERA

(in millions of pesos)

	Net Profits	Paid-in Capital	Dividends
1934......	0.4	20.3	0.1
1940......	0.8	7.9	0.5
1941......	1.8	8.0	0.6
1945......	5.0	11.4	0.9
1950......	16.0	100.0	6.1
1955......	48.0	200.0	13.4
1956......	108.0	200.0	n.a.

Economic Results

The Combined Mexican Working Party, reporting on the impact of the Nacional Financiera as of 1950, noted that

> data are lacking which would permit an accurate enumeration of Nacional Financiera's financial contributions to Mexico's industrial

development. . . . Nacional Financiera's net contribution to the industrial sector between 1946 and 1950 fluctuated from a low of 3.4% in 1946 to a high of 9.0% in 1947, averaging 6.9% for the period as a whole. However, the total investment of the enterprises aided by Nacional Financiera would be a higher proportion of over-all industrial investment, if account were taken of industry's repayments to Nacional Financiera and the fact that the agency's financial assistance probably amounts to less than half the total investment in the enterprises concerned . . . It must be concluded that the Nacional Financiera's contribution to Mexico's industrial development has not been very large in purely financial terms. Nevertheless by concentrating its investments and technical assistance in areas where serious shortages of supply or capital existed, Nacional Financiera was able to eliminate some important obstructions to industrial development . . . If its objectives have been too limited, or its efforts insufficient to prevent the emergence of grave distortions within the developing economy, these shortcomings can hardly be laid at the door of Nacional Financiera.

The Combined Working Party also noted that the institution's efforts were concentrated on the promotion of large-scale industries, thus leaving for the future the solution of the problem of providing technical and financial aid to small industry. [3] Since then, the Government has established a special fund for financial assistance to small enterprises, which is being administered by the Nacional Financiera.

[3] *The Economic Development of Mexico* (Baltimore, 1953), pp. 79-80.

Index